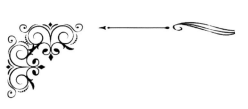

Where Patriots Rally
When Democracy Is Threatened

The Origin & History of the
Political Principles Contained in

The Declaration of Independence

Ben McNitt

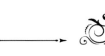

Printed in the United States of America
First Printing Edition, 2023

eBook: ISBN: 978-1-962155-09-0
Paperback: ISBN: 978-1-962155-10-6
Hardcover: ISBN: 978-1-962155-11-3

Table of Contents

Thomas Sully portrait of Thomas Jefferson
Source: Library of Congress

Prologue

American democracy is under authoritarian attack. This essay narrates the origin and history of our founding principles so that you may be better able and more inclined to defend them from that attack. As Thomas Paine, the pamphleteer of the American Revolution, put it, "These are the times that try men's souls." To be worthy of our democracy we must be willing to fight for its survival.

The object of this essay's inquiry is a set of ideas — the principles written into the Declaration of Independence — the self-evident truths of universal equality based on inalienable natural rights to life, liberty and the pursuit of happiness under governance by consent of the governed.

The essay's premise is that a basic grasp of humankind's quest to extract these principles from more than twenty centuries of hard experience can inspire a renewed dedication to them.

The attack on our democracy and its founding principles comes from an angry populist impulse toward authoritarianism. Strains of white supremacy and its handmaidens of racism and bigotry are opening up like lesions on the body politic. White working-class resentment seethes over being dealt out of the global information economy and buffeted by the rapid transformation of America's most familiar face from a monochromatic white to a starburst of color and orientation. This strain of authoritarianism relies on a deep reservoir of anti-intellectualism. Its current iteration has spawned a new language of alternative facts to support its uncoupled from reality narrative. A new post-truth language of false facts is being used to wall off believers from The Other, those on the far side of an unbreachable societal chasm. Interestingly, the language arose before the impulse matured. More than a decade ago, as of this writing, newspaper columnist Neal Gabler noted "we live in a post-Enlightenment age in which rationality, science, evidence, logical argument and debate have lost the battle in many sectors ... to superstition, faith, opinion and orthodoxy."

The central irony of the Declaration's principles is that none of them were true when written. All were not created equal. There were no self-evident truths beyond a few axioms of math. There were no inalienable rights to life, liberty, and the pursuit of happiness. Natural law was a mental emanation without statutory authority. Government legitimacy did not depend on the consent of the governed. No one had a right to revolt. The entire construct was aspirational. Any woman or Black person in white society of the era could testify they were born subservient, not equal. Countless generations of those born of the wrong gender, or color, or to serfdom, slavery, peasantry, or to any lesser position in life set for them before their birth had no concept of, much less any claim to inalienable rights to life, liberty and the pursuit of happiness. The history of millennia affirmed that the powerful rule the weak. Pharaohs, emperors, kings, prelates, and popes had nearly always, in nearly all circumstances, held their self-written title deeds to authority — either temporal or spiritual and often both together — gripped tightly in their own hands.

The Declaration's principles live because people believe them. Their power spans generations of individuals who recognized they have a direct stake in those principles as though they were, as Abraham Lincoln put it, "blood of the blood and flesh of the flesh" of the those who wrote them, a set of beliefs linking present and future generations to the nation's Founders.

The Declaration expresses America's political creed, or more accurately has become the nation's political creed. It was not intended as such. The Continental Congress did not ask delegate Thomas Jefferson and four other colleagues to prepare a document in the summer of 1776 setting out political principles to govern a new nation. Amidst a wave of revolutionary sentiment, the moment's urgent task was for a statement giving the reasons the united colonies decided to break their political ties to Great Britain — a literal declaration of independence. Jefferson's main effort, aided by his two closest collaborators Benjamin Franklin and John Adams, went to articulating twenty-nine reasons justifying the break. That bill of particulars takes up most of the document. The indictment's most distinguishing feature is that — aside from the complaint of taxation without representation — it is the least remembered or cited portion of the document.

The opening stanza's Biblical intonation of *When in the course of human events,* and the second paragraph's assemblage of what were then widely shared political convictions are a flourish, like fireworks on the Fourth of July.

Congress spent little time on them when the draft was submitted for review. But they stuck. They were a constant remonstrance to slaveholders written by a slaveholder until slavery was defeated. Lincoln turned to them at Gettysburg to define a Civil War fought so that government of, by and for the people shall not perish from the earth. Millions of people over decades of struggle have fought to have themselves included within the Declaration's embrace of universal equality.

The Declaration's statement of self-evident truths set the precedent for founding a nation upon a creed. Today's authoritarian assault is aimed at that creed. Tribal allegiance challenges universal equality just as the urge for The Leader to settle all accounts threatens self-government.

This should hardly be surprising. The Declaration's creed has too often been mistaken as the culmination rather than as an exception to Western political experience. Monarchial government from the early civilizations of the Fertile Crescent and the Nile River underwent shifts in form, but essentially not in content from Greece and Rome through the Middle Ages and up to the American and French revolutions of the late 18th century. The government that Western and Mediterranean civilization has known, with rare and temporary exceptions, has been that of concentrated power in a top sliver of society and subjugation, peasantry, serfdom and slavery for the masses. Authoritarianism has been the default basis for nearly all forms of government in the West for the past 7,000 years. In most cases authoritarianism was held to be supernaturally ordained. Despotism — from benign to tyrannical — is the primary narrative of Western political existence. Representative government, and rule by social compact involving the participation and consent of the governed, have no guarantee of a secure future. They are, rather, a recent outlier in history and perhaps a transitory one. Globally, democratic norms have lost ground to authoritarianism for over a decade. This is in part true because authoritarian government requires only submission enforceable by the state's coercive powers, while democracy requires work — awareness, engagement, agreement on basic sets of facts, tolerance, compromise, and a willingness to accept defeat so long as a chance for future victory exists.

Authoritarianism is a state of existence. Democracy is a job.

At this point, I need to acknowledge a central truth in all that follows: virtually every word cited is the work of long-dead white men. On reflection the thought must arise that it is preferable to learn from and participate in a framework of actual equality rather than a feigned version of it. We need no more than to recall the Declaration's actual words are "all men are created equal." The universal application of that concept is of more recent vintage. The problem with the Founders, and most of those upon whose shoulders they stood, is that the boundaries of freedom they defined essentially only included themselves. This is an obvious limitation. It need not be a barrier.

"We have it in our power to begin the world over again," Thomas Paine said of the revolutionary expectations that abounded in 1776 America. Paine was an incendiary whose essay *Common Sense* catalyzed the argument for revolt in sharp vernacular accessible to all. Packaged within his brief sentence were two millennia of human endeavor in the West to understand and shape the world: a catalogue of questioning, occasional brilliance, religious stricture and dissent, struggle, imprisonment, torture, war, and pain of every conceivable dimension, and the consequences of all that. Nearly two-hundred-fifty years on, we sense but a shadow of the drama, risk, and exultance that were alive in that era. Tracing back the origins of Jefferson's brief assemblage of principles is tied up in all but forgotten historical obscurities. Caught up in finally arriving at Jefferson's pen were responses to the questions of the nature of reality, the individual's status in society, the ends of reason, and the legitimacy of religion's temporal sway. Even astronomy played its part. Optical inventions not only probed the solar system's planetary scheme, they also prompted questions about institutional tyranny over human minds. If the Catholic Church's insistence on an Earth-centered universe could literally be observed to be false, then what other dogmas might be questionable?

Some of the Declaration's most fervent believers shroud it with an aura its authors never intended. God intervened to guide America's founding, according to this doctrine, giving inspiration to Thomas Jefferson just as surely as he did to Paul of Tarsus. The Declaration's charting the farthest then-known boundary of human reason's definition of self-governance was a deliberately non-religious act. Seeing it as divinely dependent dissolves its actual meaning. The Declaration is the fruit of human reason, not divine revelation.

Critics have dismissed the Declaration as both mistake and myth. The height of presumption, this line of argument runs, is to found a nation on a creed that its citizens may or may not recognize. That mistake is compounded by using the Declaration as proof of American exceptionalism. This myth of self-importance, critics hold, has justified rolling over other peoples and cultures on this continent, in the eventual creation of global empire. America's creation story of Manifest Destiny is written in conquest. Abuse of the concept of being a champion of freedom does not make freedom unworthy of being championed.

This essay strives to present the Declaration's principles as they were first articulated, then sifted and adapted over the course of Western history. They can be seen as ideals, but that conception misstates the essence. The Declaration's self-evident truths are intended to be understood in those terms — they are presented as principles the Founders held to be demonstrably true, the distillation of reason applied to the human condition over time. Religious belief plays a continuing role, sometimes as guide, others as barrier. Reason, however, the human capacity to logically extract principles from experience, is the prime mover. The grist from this mill is elegantly simple.

If you accept that the pursuit of happiness is expressive of our core principles it follows that one cannot pursue happiness without being free, that life and liberty are prerequisites of that pursuit, just as a society governed by the consent of the governed is a prerequisite of liberty.

To seek happiness as life's object is the simplest and most enduring answer yet offered to humankind's most complex and enduring questions of Why are we here and How should we live our lives? That pursuit may take different paths — to seek the golden mean, or personal ambition, or spiritual enlightenment. The Declaration includes the pursuit of happiness among a short list of what are called natural rights, without any claim to ultimate purpose. Presumably, that may be decided by free individuals. Jefferson chose and the Continental Congress agreed to use the foundation stone of pursuit of happiness over that of a natural right to own property. Perhaps the reason was the refreshing brashness of placing human happiness over a right to property. More certainly Jefferson, and other members of Congress, had reservations about property ownership. Does property include human beings? May it rightfully be an oligarchic Trojan Horse within a democracy? Can it include that which is needed by all but is owned by a few? The two concepts have their own history of origin, but the pursuit of happiness dates back farthest in time.

Universal equality has a parallel in biblical teaching of the equality of all in the eyes of God. The Declaration invokes an equality among individuals in the here and now, a shared status of each person's equal claim to the natural rights belonging to all — rights to free speech, belief, assembly, and even revolt among them. In principle, the assertion of equality shattered inherited or consigned status with the understanding that while outcomes would certainly differ, no one was born superior or inferior to any other one. We measure today how far short of that standard we fall, or how much closer we have come to attaining it. Linked to liberty — freedom of action that does not intrude on the freedom of others — the two concepts posit a society of individuals who in a very real sense precede the government, who determine the government and for whom the government is intended as servant, not master. These ideas were revolutionary. In nearly all previous history, government was simply the administrative arm of the person who had physical control over a swath of territories that might change by inheritance, compact, murder or conquest. The concept of 'the state' did not exist until late in the process. For the most part, the ruler was the state. The individual's role was to serve the ruler, to perpetuate his reign. The Declaration flipped this construct on its head. The government now was to serve the individual. In this process the Declaration became a living document. It falls to each generation to define the scope and depth of equality and liberty. Or to do otherwise.

The Declaration envisioned that, in Paine's words, "a whole new world is at hand."

Plato, pointing up to the sky, on left, and Aristotle, gesturing down toward Earth, on right, in Vatican mural by Raphael. Source: Picryl

The Ancient Greeks

New Testament readers are familiar with the Golden Rule from Matthew 7:12 — Do unto others as you would have them do unto you. This admonition from Christ's Sermon on the Mount dates back beyond the mists of recorded history. Christ is said to have attributed it to the law of the Hebrew prophets.

As a guide to reciprocal conduct, the Golden Rule is the oldest sketch of a social contract in human history. Within it the weak are collectively protected from abuse by the strong and the strong reap the benefits of a peaceful society. The Golden Rule is a pledge of mutual advantage not to harm one another by protecting all from being harmed. A second rule follows closely on its heels: to give to a person what is due to that person. We call this justice — to render that which is due, either in the form of reward or punishment. Both ideas fit comfortably into our modern context however often in the breach.

The Stoic philosophers of ancient Greece are credited with the earliest inquiries into natural law. Their concept of natural law is based on human reason. Something kept the universe from disintegrating into chaos. Something kept it whole, imparting continuity and often sublime harmony. The earliest Mediterranean civilizations devoted lavish sacrifices to their gods so that they might keep it that way. The Stoics posited that nature itself must be ruled by inherent natural laws that could be discerned by human reason. "Our natures are part of the nature of the universe," the Stoic Chrysippus wrote. "Therefore, the goal becomes 'to live following nature,' that is according to one's own nature and that of the universe." In a world reflecting universal principles of reason, the laws needed to reflect the same principles. A law contrary to reason, the Stoics held, should be rejected.

This marked a wholly new rationale for governance that cleared away superstition, ritual, and incantations in favor of applying reason to how society should operate. Aristotle reflected Stoic thinking when he wrote "For there really is, as everyone to some extent divines, a natural justice and injustice that is common to all." Through the application of natural law, applied uniformly to all citizens, a space was created in which all free men were equal. The Stoics greatest contribution to future generations was in identifying that space and attributing it to natural law. "God made all men free," the philosopher Alcidamas wrote in the 4th century BCE, "nature has made no man a slave." The Greeks, of course, thrived on slavery. Ancient Athens depended upon it just as later did Rome. Both societies' reckoning of rights was a discussion among men who could claim citizenship to one of the great cities.

The pursuit of happiness also makes its way onto the stage during the era of Athenian democracy that endured for nearly two centuries until sixteen years after the Macedonian conquest of 338 BCE. Both Plato and his student Aristotle held that a life dedicated to virtue was rewarded with an

12

individual state of well-being termed *eudaimonia* or happiness. Some decades earlier the philosopher Democritus urged the virtuous life as the surest way to happiness. Virtue, in turn, is comprised of such qualities as wisdom, courage, temperance and justice. To live by virtue meant fulfilling one's potential in life. "The goal of man from the start is to be happy," Aristotle wrote, and "it is virtuous activities that determine our happiness." Thomas Jefferson adopted this view, guided by his own experience and his study of the Greek masters.

Before the modern era began, Mediterranean cities — Athens being not the only democracy in Greece — practiced and grappled with key principles that found their way into the Declaration some 2,000 years later. The pursuit of happiness as life's goal was perhaps the most widely accepted. Frameworks of social contract and natural law emerged. Consent of the governed who as (male) citizens were equal under the law shown for a brief but memorable period of time. Behind these concepts lay their motivating force — they were the work of citizens, not kings or priests; they relied on human reason, not religious dogma. They were standards by which men could measure themselves.

Seen through the broadest lens, the Greeks can be said to have captured the Declaration's essence roughly 2,000 years before Jefferson wrote its now famous opening lines. Follow me, if you will, on these steps. Justice — giving one one's due regardless of gender — is the greatest good. A life lived with justice along with virtue and knowledge leads to happiness. Life and liberty are one's due under justice.

Therefore, justice — the supreme good — endows one with rights to life, liberty and the pursuit of happiness.

These ideas competed with many others. Plato, for instance, was no fan of democracy. He thought it a formula for "destructive chaos." His ideal, expressed in *The Republic*, was for an august body of philosophers and a select band of warriors to lead and defend the mass of society from farmers to artisans. Structure, not freedom, was the proper refuge against life's vicissitudes.

Plato lived from 428 to 348; Aristotle, his famed student, from 384 to 322, both Before the Common Era. Like many brilliant students, Aristotle rejected his teacher's core messages. He believed emphatically that deductive reasoning was key to revealing nature's secrets. Reasoning by syllogism may be his greatest contribution to human understanding. In its most simplified sense this is the argument that if A equals B and B equals C then A equals C. As simple as this sounds, in the minds of obsessive logicians it can open a rabbit hole into calculating how many angels can dance on the head of a pin. That is essentially what happened for many hundreds of years when scholasticism — another name for Aristotelian reasoning — dominated Europe's centers of learning throughout the late Middle Ages. The method led to impenetrable rigidity of thought, a sclerosis of the mind excluding innovation, nuance, and original thinking. Everything became derivative, in lock-step with accepted maxims.

Aristotle also developed the concept of the golden mean, that in politics he described as a balancing point between pure democracy and absolute monarchy. This idea became especially useful centuries later as debate emerged about what the structure of government might look like if built on that principle.

The Prime Mover or Unmoved Mover, the proposition of a creator of the universe separate and distinct from all the physical things in the universe, comes directly from Aristotle. The Catholic Church eventually welcomed this as a validation of its worldview from among the greatest of the ancient philosophers.

Aristotle's vision of the universe had profound repercussions during the historical turning point nearly twenty centuries later when the certainties of religious doctrine were questioned by observable fact. Prior to the Greeks, the universe had been described as the domain of Babylonian star gods or of Egypt's god of the sun who renewed himself each morning for his transit of the sky. That changed as Greek-influenced rationalism took hold. Aristarchus, a near contemporary of Aristotle, conjured a theory that the sun and the fixed stars were immovable with the sun at the universe's center, and the Earth revolving around it once every year while rotating on its own axis once every day. The idea, however brilliant, flared out with only rare scraps of manuscripts left to speak for it.

Aristotle conjured the same question with a far different result. His theory shared much in common with Plato's teachings. If one posits that nature is perfect, as he did, that it contains no mistakes, then one can deduce that a perfect circle is a reflection of nature's perfection. Imposing this rule required that the then observable planets follow perfectly circular orbits. Allowing his conclusion to dictate the facts, Aristotle worked out a system of fifty-four spheres within spheres to create a physical model of creation. To kick the machine into operation, Aristotle placed his Unmoved Mover at the outermost sphere with all the inner spheres, excepting that of the Earth and moon, being realms of unchangeable perfection.

The degradation of imperfection was relegated to earth's human sphere. This was his proposition. Later scholastic thinkers ossified it into unquestionable dogma. Aristotle placed the Earth at the center of the universe as did Plato. Scholastics ossified that into dogma, too.

Natural law continued as an historical through-line, as we shall see, up to the time Jefferson wrote of nature's law bestowing an endowment of inalienable rights. The Greeks left fertile fields of later inquiry over such issues as the best form of government, innate equality, the meaning of happiness, and much else as well.

However, another aspect of Plato's teaching in particular had a profound impact on early Christianity and by extension our inquiry into the Declaration's principles.

The subject was the invisible, that which can be imagined but not seen.

The context was the struggle among competing sects for primacy in the nascent world of early Christianity. Catholicism did not achieve orthodoxy over rival interpretations of Christ's teachings until some 300 years after his crucifixion. Marcionites who posited competing gods of good and evil vied for attention with Gnostics who created a nearly impenetrable world of ecstatic revelation and secret learning. The seekers of Christ's legacy included Jewish-Christian Ebionites who demanded adherence to Hebraic law, and Carpocratians who proclaimed the transmigration of souls. Some believed Christ was created by God and was thus subordinate to him. Others believed Christ was born human and only later did God adopt him. This is to say nothing of the mass of gentiles who worshiped beings ranging from the denizens of Mt. Olympus to spirits of the forests.

Early church fathers understandably were open to argument that helped make their case. Scripture held accounts and interpretations of one man's life. They did not present a cosmology, a unified conception of the universe and humankind's place in it.

Plato did. His writings and their rendering by later disciples like the Egyptian-born philosopher Plotinus and the early church father Origen, who was tortured for his faith, provided a structure not found in Scripture. That the message came from one of the most distinguished scholars of antiquity whose wisdom seemed a prevision of Christianity was a major added bonus.

Take the Trinity for example. This is the creed of Father, Son and Holy Spirit that the 325 Council of Nicaea adopted as Catholic doctrine — the three manifestations of God. Plato prefigured the concept by positing a hierarchy rendered variously as the One, Mind, and Soul, or the Good, Intelligence and World Soul. For Plato these were all a sort of primal radiance that later Catholic leaders discerned as a parallel to the Trinity.

Monotheism provided another doctrinal similarity. In springing from its Hebrew heritage Catholicism propounded the existence of the one true God. Interestingly, instead of recognizing Greek mythology as anything but that, Plato was among the first to posit a unitary God. In his version a manifestation of this God, or the One, was the Demiurge, the benevolent entity who shaped and composed the physical world, not unlike Aristotle's Prime Mover. Catholic theologians recognized a kinship on this point as long as one did not read the fine print too closely.

Other examples could be cited. However, the most convincing resonance is in Plato's formulation of his unique conception of Forms. Here we enter a transcendental realm, a world of the incorporeal that Plato deemed was vastly superior to the material world of everyday life. Put simply, that's Catholicism's wheelhouse — the mystery of faith in a God beyond human conception or description. Plato provided a language to describe the mystery that could not be found in Scripture.

Plato sought knowledge, pure, incorruptible, permanent knowledge. He was certain such understanding could not be found in the ever-changing impermanence of the material world. So, he created his own hypothetical world that he posited was located on a Plain of Truth existing beyond the realm of human senses. This ethereal universe was dominated by his theory of Forms. In fact, Plato argued, studying, and attempting to comprehend the Forms was vastly more important than study of all that could be seen or touched. The invisible was beyond measure superior to the visible. A horse that you ride, even the finest steed, or a perception of beauty that you see, even of the highest order, are shadows, imitations, mimicry of the true Form they represent. A legal ruling may strive to achieve justice, but no human determination can encompass the true Form of Justice that exists in the Plain of Truth. Forms are the essence of a higher reality. Observable reality is a shadow of its Form. In adopting this stance, Plato rejected scientific inquiry as not only less meaningful, but also as a diversion from that which was truly meaningful.

The Good is the highest Form, the progenitor of all other Forms and their worldly analogs. The beneficence with which the good overflows was readily seen in Christian eyes as prefiguring God's abundance of love. All things in life that are good — beauty and justice and courage as examples — are mere remnants of the greater reality of the ineffable, unobtainable, indescribable Form of The Good. God could be seen in such formulations.

Plato also provided a hierarchy of Forms with the Good as the emanating force, perfect and immutable at the pinnacle of existence. Life's highest object was to deeply contemplate the Good as a pathway to life's virtues of justice, temperance, and happiness, just as in Catholicism life's purpose was to worship God as the pathway to eternal life. On the hierarchy's lowest rung lay the changeable and degraded plane of humankind, compelled to look upward for a sign of salvation.

What does all this have to do with the Declaration?

Of all the pathways the ancient Greeks opened for exploration the one most readily adopted by their Christian inheritors was the world of mystery beyond the tangible, a world in which all that could be seen, handled, measured and described gave way to worship of what could be sensed but not seen.

It was as if Western humanity deliberately placed a blindfold over its eyes to see more clearly. This intellectual handoff dispensed with all the talk about democracy, happiness, equality, natural laws and those other things that comprise the Declaration's principles.

Augustine of Hippo. Imaginative portrait
by Philippe de Champaigne. Source: Picryl

Augustine of Hippo

From atop the combined church and monastery on a hill within the North African harbor city of Hippo, the Mediterranean Sea stretched north to the horizon. In the plains encircling the rest of the city olive groves and vineyards fit in among large fields of corn. Lions were hunted in the mountains to the south.

Hippo was a prosperous Roman city. In the year 395 it welcomed the ordination of a new Catholic Bishop who had already served several years there as a priest. Augustine of Hippo, as he was known, was forty-one years old upon his ordination. He remained there until he died thirty-five years later, possibly of starvation, as an invading band of Vandals besieged and finally overran the outpost of a once great empire.

As he is now known to the world, St. Augustine has had a more profound impact on Western orthodox religion even up to the present than any other person since Paul of

Tarsus. His teachings truncated Western political development for over a thousand years by burying it under the supernatural world of his faith.

The City of God is Augustine's masterwork describing every niche of orthodox religious belief. He started it in the year 413 in response to the 410 sack of Rome. His magnificently achieved object was to present a coherent schema of life dedicated to the glory of the Catholic Church rising from the Roman world's ashes. The church had a foothold in Western civilization in Augustine's time. Roughly seven hundred years later it reached its full eminence.

Hippo, now known as the Algerian city of Annaba, was diverse. Romans, most of them nominally Catholic since Emperor Constantine had embraced the cross in the year 312, mixed with pagans who worshiped traditional gods, native Berbers, Manicheans, Donatists and a scattering of seafarers and merchants from around the Mediterranean rim. Augustine had himself embraced Manichaeism. Mani, the sect leader, taught faith in a cosmic conflict between the good of the spiritual world of light and the evil of the material world of darkness. After holding to the sect for a decade, Augustine abandoned it, ultimately finding his home in the true faith in which he experienced an ecstatic epiphany of a "flash of a trembling glance" of eternal beauty. He was born again. Augustine's relationship with the Donatists was fraught. This sect demanded that priests be unblemished if their conduct of church ritual was to be valid. With some coercion that left sect members dead, Augustine helped drive the Donatists out of Hippo.

The Donatists concern reflected a wider reality as Christianity overtook the pagan gods of Rome and its diverse territories. The pantheon of Greek and Roman gods could be appeased or persuaded by ritual. They did not dictate personal behavior or ethics. Judeo-Christian traditions do. From the Ten Commandments through Deuteronomy, the Sermon on the Mount, St. Paul's letters and the latest Papal Bull these religious confessions bring a host of prescriptive doctrine. Sex is closely regulated — at least in theory. Doctrine decides who can have sex with whom just as it distinguishes between those sexual practices that are allowed and those that are forbidden. During Christianity's first 1,500 years, in particular, the answers to such questions as who rules and who obeys, how to avoid harsh judgment and to merit an eternal reward, what a person may or may not read, or may or may not say along with scores of other ethical and moral questions were answered by prelates who best understood God's will. Ultimately those who wrote and enforced these rules used them to rule over those for whom they were written.

Modern readers can have but a dim perception of St. Augustine's world. The Bishop of Hippo had no insight into the cosmos' immensity and violence. Within his mind's grasp, the Earth was placed at the center of everything. God placed it there to benefit the human race he created in his own image to follow a divine plan of punishments and rewards. At the plan's climax everything on Earth would be destroyed except for those select individuals he chose to reside with him in heaven for eternity. Augustine believed that human bodies that had been dismembered, burned, or allowed to rot could magically restored to fullness and health, ascended to heaven and be blessed to live there forever without nourishment. The material universe consisted entirely of what could be seen and no more. Augustine himself thought the Earth was about 6,000 years old.

Like Plato, what mattered most to Augustine was what could not be seen. His inner-vision was a world of supernatural phenomena that influenced or determined literally everything that occurred in the material world. The Roman and other pagan gods, Augustine believed, were not myths but real beings, probably "unclean spirits and malignant demons."

Invisible demons beset Augustine and his world. He wrote page after page about whether good demons exist, how to define them, if they could mediate between humans and God, and if men's souls can become demons. He was equally concerned about angels, good and bad ones, about where they came from and if God authored the nature of good angels.

Taken literally, Augustine's God is remarkably similar to the recent theory that all life and existence are no more than the playing out of an enormous computer program. We are all a computer simulation. In Augustine's case, God's mind is the computer, his will is the program. Augustine's God is co-extensive with literally everything on earth, all life, and all matter. Every pattern of waves on the sea, every storm, fire, earthquake or drought, every flight path of every bird and every sparrow that falls, all these and everything more down to the tiniest detail expresses God's direct determination or his divine permission.

In Augustine's world God is not an observer checking off what one does right and wrong on destiny's ledger sheet. God is in your mind and in your body, fully present in everything, everywhere and always. He is like some sort of dark energy that exists everywhere but is nowhere detectable by human senses — except perhaps in a fleeting, blinding flash of insight that only the slightest few ever experience.

Next, add to this construct that God has foreknowledge of everything. In fact, God may not only have had foreknowledge of every person's life, thoughts and actions, but that he may well have had such foreknowledge before he created the universe. At the very least, Augustine argues that God has complete foreknowledge of every person's life before that person is born. This sets up the conundrum of why God would choose to observe everything as it is actually occurring when he has already long known what will occur. Does this mean that prayers, say, for an ill friend are worthless because the outcome was determined long ago? Or does the outcome reflect God's foreknowledge of those prayers? Space and time begin to drift from any moorings. Because in his perfection God cannot do any evil, it follows that earthquakes, fires, plagues and floods must reflect God's displeasure at something humans have done that was known to God before they did it. Reasoned cause and effect disintegrate into God's mysterious and unknowable design. Augustine does carve out a place for free will in a way that distinguishes his version of foreknowledge from that of absolute predetermination. Again, because God is perfect, Augustine argues he cannot direct humankind to do evil. They do that themselves. "A man does not sin unless he wills to sin," Augustine wrote. Rather "the sole origin of evil is the free choice of the will."

The dichotomy between Augustine's godly realm of perfection and humankind's infliction of evil upon itself reflects Plato's sphere of the perfect form of The Good on the one hand and his lowest sphere of disorder inhabited by humans on the other. Plato's highest form could neither be seen nor comprehended but enlightened those who devoted study to it. The same was true of the unfathomable world of God and his deepest mystery of the Holy Trinity. Augustine channeled Plato, thereby adding a gloss of vindication for Christianity provided by an illustrious Greek philosopher who was revered in much of the gentile world. In Augustine's era less than half of those living within territory nominally claimed by Rome were Christian. Recruitment to orthodoxy was a means of survival. "There are none who come nearer to us than the Platonists," Augustine believed. The Roman Catholic church held to that belief until the long-lost works of Aristotle were resurrected nearly 1,000 years later. That occurrence, that we will visit, marked a turning point in doctrine under the next towering Catholic teacher St. Thomas Aquinas.

Augustine also had a great deal to say about the human condition. It was grim. His starting point was that "nobody in this flesh, nobody in this corruptible body, nobody on the face of this earth, in this malevolent existence, in this life full of temptation — nobody can live without sin." That fate was sealed by the original sin of defying God's will in the Garden of Eden. That was the first time a human used free will to commit evil. The evil was so profound, Augustine taught, that all humankind — including those who never even heard of Christ and the Scriptures — were up to the final generation cursed by Adam and Eve's original transgression. He lamely wrote that those who were condemned to hell even though they were ignorant of the Christian message, perhaps "will burn more gently." That curse, however, need not condemn one to an eternity of hellfire. Even a life of sin could be met with God's reward of salvation. That reward was granted solely as a gift of God's grace. It matters not whether one lives a righteous or a sinful life, God bestows his grace solely as an act of divine kindness. Admittedly, Augustine argues, one can and should live so as to deserve God's grace, but God can never be placed in a position of owing it to anyone. At all events, in Augustine's mind the chances of salvation were exceedingly small. Many were called but few are chosen. Hell was humankind's default destination.

"All men, as long as they are mortals, must needs be also wretched," is Augustine's epitaph for humanity.

In Augustine's view, the material world itself was not worth much either. Nature was God's "dumb show." Devotion to contemplating God so one might experience his "ineffable sweetness" was far superior than "to probe into the nature of things." Repeating text from St. Paul's letters, Augustine warned, "Take care that no one leads you astray by philosophy and useless misleading teaching, based on elements of the world." No profit was to be had, Augustine believed, "from investigating the realm of Nature." For hundreds of years thereafter many monks and priests proudly proclaimed their ignorance of the physical world that they spurned in their devotion to a spiritual one.

Any brief survey of Augustine's influence on the Western mind must include his attitude toward sex. He was obsessed by it, or more to the point "the lust that excites the indecent part of our body." He was merely following St. Paul's teaching, but with a vengeance. *City of God* is replete with references such as the "disgusting acts too filthy to be named," and the "indecent postures" of "the techniques of vice." It may fairly be argued that no person who has ever lived did more than Augustine to scar the minds of believers with a sense of self-loathing and sexual guilt.

More pertinent to our inquiry is Augustine's attitude toward who has a right to rule over others in the material world. As he often did, he drew from St. Paul for an answer. His conclusion echoed through the centuries as the divine right of kings, the defense of things as they were rather than as they might be, a yoke that bound people to monarchy, benign or despotic.

It's worth taking a moment to examine Paul's teaching about legitimate rule. The pertinent passage comes from his letter to Romans 13:1-2: "Let every soul be subject to the governing authorities. For there is no authority except from God, and the authorities that exist are appointed by God. Therefore, whoever resists the authority resists the ordinance of God, and those who resist will bring judgment on themselves."

Paul of Tarsus wrote, or more likely dictated, this letter in about the year 55. His object was to guide a small group of believers living in the hostile environment of pagan Rome's imperial power. Christians were persecuted there, as later was Paul himself. They practiced their faith in secret, most often in private homes where they came together for a meal and worship out of sight of the Empire's agents. The days of an orthodox canon called the New Testament, a Saint Paul, or a Catholic Pope in Rome were centuries off. One of Paul's primary aims was to keep his flock from being destroyed. He urged them not to rock the boat. He counsels them not to challenge authority. When Paul composed his letter, the supreme authority was the emperor Nero who ultimately blamed the Christians for burning Rome. We cannot know Paul's state of mind as he was writing. To posit that this itinerant preacher of the imminence of apocalypse and the urgency of salvation wrote a couple of lines about authority intending that they be like an ordinance of God unto the final generation is preposterous. The urgency of Paul's message was shaped by his conviction that the End Times were at hand. He was not writing for future generations. He did not think there would be any. It matters not. As part of Scripture, for believers Paul's letters bear the imprint of God's will. The consequences of all this are hysterically out of proportion to any original intent.

In one of the most cynical of his messages, Augustine — a man revered for his insights into God's essential goodness — wrote "As far as this mortal life is concerned, which is spent and finished in a few days, what difference does it make under what rule a man lives who is soon to die, provided only that those who rule him do not compel him to what is impious and wicked."

In Augustine's mind rational thought disappears in an immersion into a world of pure faith. Things one can see and touch become less real than faith guided by God's unfathomable will. By the same token, things that cannot be seen or touched like spirits, demons and angels become palpably real. One is left in a phantasmagoria of imagination. The ethereal is material, the material is evanescent. A human life has barely a speck of meaning given its mere flicker of existence in the immensity of eternity. Suffering is to be endured. Calamities are God's righteous punishments. The individual's role is to seek God and obey. For the majority, the reward of life is eternal hell. Discussions of freedom and liberty do not flourish in these conditions.

Undoubtedly many of Augustine's parishioners enjoyed sex, viewed belief as a sort of insurance policy paid by premiums of showing up to mass on occasion, maybe even taking communion once a year, and having some due regard for not condemning their souls to hell. Many parishioners are like that today just as many do try to walk in Christ's footsteps.

Augustine prescribed a complete framework for belief that lasted for an epoch just when Rome was fading, and the Church became ascendant. It was as though the rational Western mind was buried under a Vesuvian load of suffocating theology. Western civilization required more than 1,000 years to dig its way back out into sunlight.

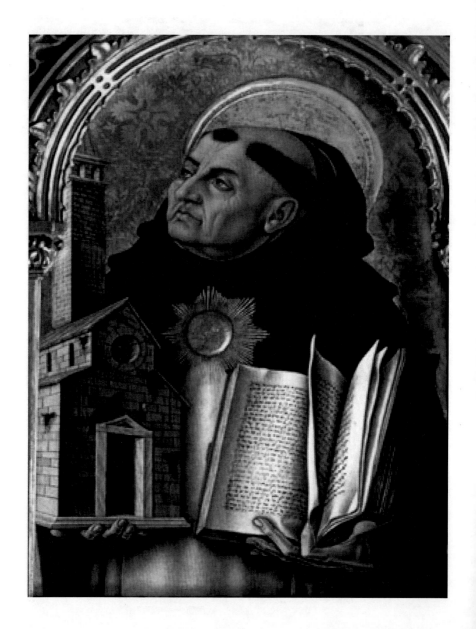

St. Thomas Aquinas who tried to reconcile faith and reason.
Portrait by Carlo Crivelli. Source: Wikimedia

Aquinas

The Western world had a lot to sort out once the Roman Empire collapsed.

Over several centuries, now best known as the Dark Ages, tribes and ethnic groups staked out something beginning to resemble the boundaries of today's Europe. Teutonic warlords plotted, inter-married and fought their way into beehives of mini-kingdoms. The Franks produced Charlemagne who produced an Empire that the philosopher Voltaire later observed was neither Holy nor Roman. Peasants spent more time placating local spirits who lurked in the mists and the forests than at church services they might attend once in any given year. A fog of suspicion, dread and superstition hung over the land like a shroud over a body.

The era merged into three currents — the rise of the Catholic Church filling the vacuum of Rome's implosion, a default to Roman imperial law where no real substitute existed and feudalism's evolution.

Once Emperor Constantine made Christianity the state religion in 313, the Catholic Church's tendrils spread along the Roman Empire's vast network of power. Augustine's bishopric in North Africa was a part of that trend. When Rome's power receded, the Church became the only coextensive authority in its place. Islam disrupted the boundaries, sweeping across the southern Mediterranean's formerly Roman enclaves and by the year 711 extended into what is now southern Spain. Further disruption came with the division of spheres of influence between Rome and Constantinople that ultimately produced the Great Schism of 1054 between the Roman Catholic and the Eastern Orthodox churches. But from England to southern Italy, and the Atlantic to the indistinct borders of what became Russia's western frontier, the Roman church began its rise to eminence. Its monasteries were virtually the only source for higher education to supply the ministers, judges and administrators required by monarchs and other elites. Kings, nobles or warlords ruled common people, but their spiritual direction for the right path in life came from but one source. Their instruction in life's ultimate rewards and punishments was the exclusive province of the one true church.

In addition to the Catholic Church, Roman law outlived the empire that created it. The church benefited because the late imperial legal code buttressed autocratic rule from the top. Plato's Forms mirror a Catholic construct of God's world allied with Roman statutes to provide the church with ready-made intellectual and legal frameworks of justification and control. For a moment in time faith was triumphant. Those who accepted Plato relied on faith because the truth resided beyond vision, touch or human description. Only faith provided hope of salvation, no matter how slim. Faith was the object of life.

Then reason was rediscovered.

The idea of right reason being key to natural law had been around, as we have seen, at least since the Stoics of ancient Greece. Its essence is that human reason can set legal parameters for society. More than that, right reason (the power of reason used correctly) will reach roughly the same conclusions across time and cultures. That the punishment should fit the crime or that one who breaks a contract is liable for damages are examples of criminal and civil natural law derived from right reason. Three of the Ten Commandments (on murder, theft and false witness) reflect natural law before Moses brought the tablets down from Mt. Sinai. Strictly speaking, right reason and natural law do not require divine intervention. An exception applies for those who hold that reason is a gift from God, an attribute of the divine in whose image humans are created. More on that in a moment and later when we look at the Declaration's premise that mankind has inalienable rights "endowed by their Creator."

Light began to penetrate the Dark Ages when the West discovered the East's legal code of the Emperor Justinian. Justinian ruled the Eastern Roman Empire beginning in 527 from Constantinople. One of his first decrees ordered the legal code to be rewritten to bring it up to date and eliminate confusion and contradiction. That took several years. At the time the lands within what had been the Western Roman Empire paid little attention and the code slipped into the mists of history there.

Beginning in the year 1070 part of the code's ten books turned up in the West in Greek versions soon translated into Latin. The core of the discovery was not so much the specific laws themselves, nor the legal precedents upon which they were based. The breakthrough was that the code was what has been called "written reason," natural law framed as a universal principle of rationality.

The next breakthrough was like the first, relearning what had been learned, and then forgotten. Searching through Arabic texts on the bookshelves of libraries in Toledo, Spain, Gerand of Cremona in 1140 made the first of many discoveries of books that had been translated into Arabic in Baghdad and Damascus from the original Greek of Euclid and Aristotle. They wound up in Toledo during the Moorish occupation of Spain. The single flame of Platonic thought that had survived through the centuries in the West became a panoply of lights once the ancient sources were recovered.

The resultant intellectual jolt was as profound as the spiritual jolt provided by understandings of Christ's life. The origin of the Italian Renaissance dates from these discoveries. A mania arose to scour likely monastic libraries for more such riches. Euclid, Galen and Aristarchus with their insights into mathematics, medicine, and cosmology were revived. So too was Aristotle.

Aristotle championed reasoned deduction based on physical evidence over his teacher Plato's Forms, the illusive truths that remained forever out of sight. His schema included a place for natural law. Simple curiosity led people — a few of the elite at first, a far wider swath of people later — to ask questions about the nature of physical reality that had no answers in Scripture.

The fervor culminated in the prolific writings of a Catholic priest named Thomas Aquinas. He took as his task to integrate Aristotelean thought including natural law into church doctrine. He made the first full-throated effort in Western history to harmonize faith and reason. In the process Plato was shunted aside. Aquinas drew a new template based on Aristotle. Under close church scrutiny the product was ultimately compressed into scholasticism, a sclerotic construct of Aristotelean inquiry.

To start with, Aristotle had the distinct advantage of positing a Prime Mover or Unmoved Mover, a force separate from the material universe that created it all. This fit nicely with the creation legend recounted in Genesis.

Several hundred years of St. Augustine's sour forecasts about life left the church in need of a less forbidding, more attractive message. Aquinas provided it. Thomism, as his doctrines came to be known, is a full-blown defense of Catholic precepts that undergird the church to this day. They also cracked open the door to modern political thinking. Reason complimented faith, he argued. Instead of being "essentially delusive," as Augustine would have it, Aquinas' view was that reason was a sign of the divine spark in all and gave humans agency in life. Natural law, he argued, was that part of God's eternal law that humans could understand and work out for themselves. One did not need Scripture to understand that theft was wrong. People could understand and describe injustice because they had experienced it. If one traced it back, the stream of natural law flowed through the Roman orator Cicero, before him to Aristotle and the Stoics, and finally back to the first admonition that has no known author to do unto others as you would have them do unto you. The legal formulation of this concept implies enforceable restrictions, to not do to others what you would not have them do to you. In Aquinas' writing, natural law belonged in a middle plane, beneath the eternal law of God but ahead of the positive laws of government. As Aquinas saw it, if in a well-governed state positive law was informed by natural law that in turn reflected divine law, then as a consequence the secular realm had moral justification rooted in the divine will.

The Catholic Church was not long in sniffing out heresy. The Church shut down university lectures on Aristotle for several years. Three years after Aquinas died in 1274, the bishop of Paris issued a proclamation that, among other things, condemned twenty Thomist propositions for violating God's omnipotence. A source of truth outside religious orthodoxy was dangerous. Until properly molded or rejected by church authority, ideas were dangerous. The church took about two hundred years to shake off its suspicions about Aristotle, but in the end, he was known simply as The Philosopher best interpreted through the Doctor and Saint of the Catholic Church, the priest Thomas Aquinas.

Catholic suspicions were well grounded. A revolutionary time bomb was embedded in the idea that people could write laws for themselves. Where might that line of thinking take you? Aquinas gave a hint when (in one of his more obscure works) he wrote that deposing an oppressive tyrant was acceptable, perhaps even desirable, if the act is carried out by the whole community and does not result in anarchy. St. Paul's blank check to rulers ordained from Heaven suddenly had a Catholic asterisk beside it. And if the people might rightly overthrow a tyrant, what about a pope who became tyrannical?

Yes, just as the people had the right to overthrow a despotic king, they also had the right to depose a tyrannical pope. So reasoned an obscure Franciscan priest from England named William of Oakham. This opinion was among those that led to his condemnation as a heretic, and exile in Bavaria where he died in about 1349.

Oakham's writings are a turning point in the history of political thought. He was among the first to deduce from natural law that applied widely to humanity as a whole, that there also must be natural rights that adhered to each individual. In Imperial Rome as well as in ancient Greece, natural law was seen as applying to society as a whole. What can be seen struggling its way into the light in Oakham was in broad context the same thing that was struggling into the light in the emergent Renaissance – the individual and all the uncharted territories that reason opened up to the individual.

Oakham is best remembered for his Razor, the maxim that all else being equal the simplest answer to a question is likely the right one. This line of thinking led him to strip away orthodoxy's accretions and presumptions to find a core of truth. For Oakham that core was the sovereignty of the people who could delegate power to a ruler or via a church council to the papacy. The people made the ultimate choice to bestow or reclaim power. The first natural right of each of them was to defend themselves from attack, including ecclesiastical overreach. A papal abuse of power was, Oakham believed, "opposed to the rights and liberties granted by God and nature." Among those rights was the freedom to own property to better protect oneself. Free speech was necessary to probe the limits of nature's laws. Oakham sketched an early version of a social contract by which people agreed to be governed: rights to self-defense, speech and property for the individual, the ability to delegate, withhold or reclaim sovereignty for the whole community. Within this structure Oakham found no justification in Scripture for papal jurisdiction in any secular matter. The church's mission was to save souls, not to administer courts or fix tax rates.

Defining power's reach was one of the great through-lines of medieval intellectual history. Popes had deployed division upon division of armed men in crusades to reclaim Jerusalem from Moslem infidels. That power faded as kings and princes found they needed those divisions to fight each other. Secular rulers and popes had recognized the need for each other from the outset but the meeting point between them was always a source of potential or actual conflict. The Knights Templar, famed defenders of the faith for their exploits during the Crusades, was wiped out in the early 1300s by King Philip IV of France. He confiscated their considerable wealth after his torturers extracted dubious Templar confessions to crimes. Templar leader Jacques de Molay was publicly burned at the stake in Paris. The Donation of Constantine, supposedly dated to the fourth century, secured the church's claim to a broad swath of secular duties and territorial jurisdictions. The church pointed to the document as Emperor Constantine's delegation to the pope and his successors of political authority over Judea, Greece, Asia, Thrace, Africa, Italy, and a clutch of Mediterranean islands. But there was a problem. In the mid-1400s a Catholic priest named Lorenzo Valla exposed the document as a fraud. It was all made up. A few years earlier the church had already gone through the debilitating embarrassment of seeing three different men each claim to be pope at the same time.

A new era was just beginning when William of Oakham put his weight on the scale. As it turned out, he was speaking for the future. The orthodox church that had defined the Western world after the Roman Empire's collapse was giving way to European monarchs and feudal princes.

Christendom was becoming Europe.

Martin Luther who chose conscience over obedience. Portrait
by Lucas Cranach the Elder. Source: Wikimedia

Reformation

The era of Reformation in Europe could be reconstructed as a nearly two-centuries-long struggle in the hearts and minds of its people over their religious convictions. That would miss the backdrop in front of which it all played out.

The era was a continuous continent-wide plunge into man's inhumanity to man driven principally by conflict over how to worship the Prince of Peace. The bloodlust with all its attendant variations was not exceeded in scale or barbarity until the 20th century's eras of Stalin, Hitler, Mao, and the bomb. War, as it always does, became more sophisticated. By 1500 mounted knights encased in armor had been replaced by massed ranks of archers and tightly packed formations of pikemen who thrust their thirteen to eighteen-foot-long weapons into their opponents' eyes, throats, guts and genitals. Dragooned peasants, prisoners, and mercenaries stocked the armies that numbered about 40,000 as the century began and grew to 150,000 when the killing ended, all expected to live off the land that brought pillage, mass rape, and devastation to their line of march. Handguns, rifles, and cannon worked their way into the ranks as the arts of war progressed.

The fervor of the times found a gruesome outlet in the refinement of torture. A surgeon in Basel was punished for blaspheming the Virgin Mary by having the flesh on his back stripped off with hot tongs before his legs and arms were amputated, his tongue was pulled out from a slash in his neck, and his body was consigned to the flames. Atrocities were common. Religious persecution, including the old standby of pogroms against the Jews, was going on somewhere against some targeted group for neigh-on two hundred years. To all this was added the occasional recurrence of the Black Plague that had been the 15th century's backdrop to life. Little wonder that hundreds of thousands fled to the less lethal uncertainties of a future in the Americas.

For most people in Europe, for the peasants, life was a trial of fear, a sort of hunched-over mentality amid a hailstorm of rocks hoping that you might somehow be saved from the near certain fate of being stoned to death. Sheer exhaustion with it all set in along with finally understanding that the conflicts' inconclusive stalemates meant that God could not have been on either side.

Something different had to happen.

Ad Fontes – Return to the Sources – was a humanist concept of Renaissance Italy that made its way to the continent just as scholars sought to escape the straitjacket of scholasticism. Its original intent was to return to recently rediscovered sources of learning from ancient Greece. In Europe it prompted a reexamination of the central source of all learning, the Bible.

The Dutch theologian Erasmus applied the concept to writing fresh translations of the New Testament in both Greek and Latin based upon original sources. He quickly encountered the problem that there were no original sources. Digging as far back as possible into the oldest New Testament manuscripts that he could find, the best he came up with were transcripts of copies of copies written a hundred years or more after the originals were set down which was usually at least a hundred years after events of Christ's life had occurred. For example, he found that a faulty translation from Hebrew to Greek may have resulted in a description of Mary as "a virgin" instead of the source's meaning of "a young woman." The greater issue was the reliability of a text attributed to God's inspiration. Even the Bible was open to question.

An obscure German priest named Martin Luther returned to Christianity's written source with a different intent that had far greater consequences. By the middle of the 1500s second decade, he became fed up with the Catholic Church's 'get out of purgatory early' passes sold by the bushel-full to finance the construction of St. Peter's Basilica in Rome. He found no scriptural justification for it. Nor could he find excuse there for the surfeit of opulence that clothed the pope, cardinals, and other prelates. Examining the text solely on its own merit, he found no basis for priests having to intermediate between believers and their god. He also found no scriptural prohibition for priests to marry. In protest against all this he proclaimed individual believers could by themselves return to the source, consult the Bible themselves to be their own priests and teachers of the way of Christ. Not only could natural law be derived from common experience, but Scripture itself was open to common understanding. The Christian faith could be found, he argued, "in the Scriptures alone." Luther stirred up a revolution now called the Reformation.

The priest from Wittenberg was short, pudgy, fearless, and vulgar. He had the instincts of a street fighter. He used words, multiplied by newly created printing presses, to excoriate, defame and slash at his opponents, as when he said of the pope and his minions that "spiritual tyrants" should be "chased away as wolves, thieves, and murderers." Citing his works as "deadly poison," the pope excommunicated Luther in 1520. In a much-delayed reaction, some of Kristallnacht's bloody-fisted Brown Shirts were inspired by his tract *On the Jews and Their Lies* that urged that synagogues and schuln be set ablaze.

When in 1522 King Charles V summoned him before a tribunal of the Holy Roman Empire to renounce his heresies, Luther changed the course of Western history. He proclaimed he would retract nothing "since it is neither safe nor right to go against conscience." He stood by these words thereby extending agency to every man and woman to abide their conscience ahead of secular decree or ecclesial edict.

With this concept, the modern era begins.

Luther's most robust assault on orthodox authority came in his *The Babylonian Captivity of the Church*. "Neither pope nor bishop nor any other man," he wrote, "has the right to impose a single syllable of law upon a Christian man without his consent." Even if one takes these words as confined to ecclesiastical disputes, they convey a radically new concept of individual liberty.

The irony is that Luther made his leap forward while reviving St. Augustine's reactionary theology. Recognizing the primacy of conscience was a foundational step in constructing the principles expressed in the Declaration. That idea held. Resurrecting Augustine meant burying human aspirations under the curse of original sin. "Through the one transgression of the one man, Adam," Luther believed, all humanity is "under sin and damnation [with] no capacity to do anything but sin and be damned." Luther's successors found a way around that.

Luther's theology centered on salvation by the grace of God completely bypassing the chits-building power the Catholic Church attributed to following ritual and performing good works. "First, God has promised certainly His grace to the humbled," Luther wrote, "that is, to the self-deploring and despairing. But a man cannot be thoroughly humbled, until he comes to know that his salvation is utterly beyond his own powers, counsel, endeavors, will, and works, and absolutely depending on the will, counsel, pleasure, and work of another, that is, of God only." Only by God's grace, he held, could one have true faith in Christ the Redeemer and be granted the eternal life that faith in Christ entailed. To be at least in line to receive God's grace, Luther wrote, "the more we judge and abhor and detest ourselves the more abundantly God's grace flows into us." Seen through a harsh lens, this translates into "Grovel. You may or may not be granted the gift of faith if you do, but by all means grovel." Public displays of men lashing themselves with whips tipped with bits of flesh-tearing metal flowed from this advice.

If this does not rob one of agency in one's salvation, Luther continues with an Augustine-style doctrine of foreknowledge.

"God foreknows all things," Luther believed. "Therefore, some are predestined to be saved, others to damnation — before they come into existence. Man, himself is completely helpless to decide the fate that has already been ordained for him." His view on free will was no less depressing. "There is no such thing as 'Free-will' at all," he wrote, trimming this slightly so as not to include mundane matters such as choices in food or clothing. But on matters touching on salvation, he held that humankind "has no 'Free-will,' but is captive, slave, and servant either to the will of God, or the will of Satan." He thus ascribes bad acts to being Satan's captive. This line of thinking raises questions like how can one be accountable for anything, particularly bad acts if one's actions are preordained by a power one has no choice but to obey. Was Judas in some way innocent of betraying Christ? Were the Nazis not responsible for the Holocaust?

By reasserting Augustinian doctrine Luther abandoned Thomas Aquinas' efforts to reconcile faith and reason and recognize a role played by natural law. In his trademark stance of absolutism, Luther declared "the sum total of all human knowledge is this: A man must know that by himself he is nothing." In a different context he wrote "To love God is to hate oneself." Taken as a whole, one might well wonder, Was Luther denying or affirming human agency in life?

These teachings may or may not have been fully embraced by those who chose Luther's Protestantism over Catholic orthodoxy. They are not particularly relevant to the principles written in the Declaration, except as obstacles to getting there. If you believe God preordained your station in life, you're not likely to be interested in liberty. What is relevant is how Luther first embraced Paul's words on God's ordination of those who hold power, and later reluctantly but clearly placed them at arm's length.

Adherence to the Pauline doctrine of the divine ordination of rulers is a sure bet that the powerless will never be anything other than powerless. Popes and rulers had used that doctrine to that end ever since Paul's first letter to Romans was made part of the New Testament canon. We have discussed earlier the utter implausibility that Paul, the evangelical preacher of the imminence of the apocalypse, could have intended his words to apply to generations he believed would never be born.

Luther's belief in this doctrine was tested during the Peasants War, a popular uprising, unsurpassed in scale until the French Revolution, that began in Germany and spread to many other parts of Europe. Though not a religious war, the rebellion was inspired by Luther's teachings and directed by the lower classes at the perceived despotism of the hierarchy of bishops and princes. Thousands of peasants were slaughtered. The rebellion did not last long. "Suffering, suffering; cross, cross," Luther responded. "O worthless Christians! ... No matter how right you are, it is not for a Christian to appeal to law, or to fight. But rather to suffer wrong and endure evil; there is no other way." As it turned out, there was another way. Over time, even Luther saw it.

As noted earlier, butchery of unprecedented proportion and duration provided the backdrop to the era. Reformation was met with Counter Reformation as religious dispute took primacy among reasons to kill. The feudal order of peasants and master was disintegrating. A class of merchants and tradesmen arose in villages that became towns and towns that grew into cities. They sought legal status more in line with their economic strength. Ancient power rivalries between princes and the church took on the added wrinkle that Protestant rulers had a new reason to grab the wealth held in Catholic hands. Emperors had vastly improved mechanisms of war to attack kings similarly armed. There was no incentive for peace.

Seams holding society together became fault lines, like tears in the fabric of life. In this context it is nearly impossible to overstate the chokehold exerted over Western society by the Pauline doctrine of divine ordination of rulers. It is not just that St. Paul wrote it in a letter to Roman congregants, or that

St. Augustine amplified it, but that rulers spiritual and secular continually called it up like a dose of a mind-numbing drug to keep the natives from becoming restless. Suffer and obey was the message of centuries of Western civilization. Resistance to the message aroused mobs and armies. It brought ostracism, excommunication, imprisonment or exile, torture of a thousand varieties, and death to one's self and possibly to one's family in another thousand varieties.

Without that resistance the Declaration could never have been written.

Some elasticity in Luther's absolutism began to show beginning in the 1530s. In elaborating the doctrine, he wrote that "foreasmuch as the temporal power has been ordained by God for the punishment of the bad and the protection of the good, we must let it do its duty." St. Paul had not written anything about temporal power being ordained to do good, or for any purpose whatsoever. God had simply ordained those who rule to rule.

Luther finally abandoned the Pauline doctrine when it came to Protestants defending themselves in a predatory war brought on by Catholics. The "murderers and bloodthirsty papists" who start war shed all legitimacy to rule, he wrote, and become "assassins and traitors" to be resisted. Instead of leading, Luther was merely catching up to an overwhelming tide of sentiment unleashed by the era's religious wars. He died in 1546 before the full ramifications of his conscience-driven break with Catholicism played out across Europe.

What was originally religious dissent increasingly took on a political edge. Justification of armed resistance took shape in the argument that any magistrate who exceeds his authority makes himself a felonious private citizen. This theory was then expanded to a constitutional argument that when a magistrate abused his authority, it became the obligation of other magistrates to resist the abuser. All the parsing of nuance should not obscure the more obvious cause and effect: when people were attacked by their rulers over confessional choices, those people fought back to escape massacre without pausing to read Paul's first letter to Romans. Theories justifying this response came after the bloodshed began. The primal natural right to self-preservation trumped all.

A case in point occurred in Paris in the summer of 1572. Catherine de Medici, the Catholic Queen Mother of France, exasperated by constant agitation from Protestant Huguenots, ordered the murder of several of their leaders. The infamous St. Bartholomew's Day Massacre ensued. Some 2,000 Huguenots were slaughtered in the city's streets before the contagion spread killing an estimated 5,000 more throughout the country. In the circumstances self-preservation quickly led to a societal level conviction that those under assault had a right, even a duty, to resist murderous tyranny forcibly. Once a religious prohibition, resistance to unjust rule became a perceived natural law and political right. Scaling this up justified revolution.

The Huguenots were followers of the French theologian John Calvin. He was even more reactionary than Luther. He embraced the Pauline doctrine of divine ordination of rulers to the bitter end. He held an utterly rigid conviction that God alone predetermined a fate of salvation or damnation for each individual. Those chosen by God were the Elect, the rest were doomed to Hell's everlasting fire. This engendered a legacy of pastoral sermons of fire and brimstone that left the faithful somewhere between motivation and traumatization. Along the way, however, Calvin's teachings were interpreted to square the circle between human agency in life and human subjugation to predetermination. This was no small trick. As presumably God's Elect were the most righteous and morally correct, then, even if the decision was not of one's own making, the more righteous and morally upright one was, the more likely one might be to be among the chosen. Given human nature, the more one acted like one of the Elect, the more one might come to actually believe one was among the Elect. The difference was empowering, creating highly motivated, morally demanding individuals who were wholly determined to do God's work in the world.

These were the people who disembarked from the Mayflower at Plymouth Rock.

They had been tempered by a life of revolution, civil war, ostracism, and exile from the old world as they entered the new. Onward Christian soldiers. Their brethren to the south were of a more adventurous stock who sought to monetize their risk for their own profit and that of their backers in England. The disruptions to life for indigenous peoples and Blacks entailed by these arrivals are integral to the broader American experience beyond the confines of this essay.

The Huguenots were a distinct minority of the French population in the late 1500s but included a sizeable portion of the nobility. Many decided to flee the country rather than suffer continual Catholic suppression. They found new homes in Sweden, Norway, and the Netherlands where the local burghers found religious toleration tended to favor their far-flung trade with the known world.

A prime destination for religious refugees lay across the English Channel. Henry VIII's 1533 break with Rome created a haven for anti-papists who became known as Puritans. In Scotland, John Knox led the Reformation creating the Presbyterian Church after Catholicism was outlawed in the country. One of Knox's associates, Christopher Goodman, helped cut not only the tie to Rome but also the tie to Paul's doctrine of rule ordained by God. When rulers become tyrants, he wrote, they shed legitimacy and in resisting them "we do not resist God's ordinance."

The English government bore the distinction of having added the innovation of rights to feudalism's reciprocal obligations centuries earlier when King Henry III grudgingly accepted the Magna Carta in 1265. The document is the foundation stone for a constitutional concept that in matters affecting the whole realm such as taxes, the king could act only with the consent of the realm. This step sprang in part from an earlier Germanic tradition that a common law resides within the people that the ruler is obliged to enforce. The English elite took the next logical step by creating a parliament by 1265. The nascent institution, initially a council of barons, opened the door to the idea of representative government. A direct link joins these developments to the American Revolution's and the Declaration's grievance of no taxation without representation some five-hundred years later.

The 1648 Peace of Westphalia is commonly cited as ending Europe's psychosis of religious war. A new conception of statehood emerged. The term had long designated the state as the lands and people under the control of a given ruler. The new understanding saw the state as consisting of the land and people within designated borders. In that light sovereignty lay with the people. Change was possible if the people demanded it. Societal structures built-up since the fall of Rome had run their course to the point of exhaustion. They did not relinquish their hold easily. At a fundamental level, the individual's rightful place in society opened up to new understandings and a different future.

Galileo Galilei. Portrait by Justus Sutarmans. Source: Picryl

Epicurus & The Scientific Enlightenment

Those seeking a glimpse of the future occasionally do so by rummaging around in the past.

A case in point is a January 1417 discovery believed to have been made in the cellar library of the Benedictine monastery in the German town of Fulda. There, as best we know, Poggio Bracciolini came upon an ancient Latin manuscript of a poem written before Christ was born. Bracciolini had once been a letter writer for the pope and was a friend of the fabulously wealthy Florentine banker Cosimo de Medici at the time of his discovery. What he discovered was *On the Nature of Things* — *De rerum natura* in Latin — a lengthy poetic rendering of the even more ancient doctrines of the Greek philosopher Epicurus.

On the Nature of Things was an early edition in what became a tidal wave of books reviving interest in long-lost works by authors of ancient Greece. Gutenberg's invention of the movable type press in about 1440 made the profusion of newly printed material possible.

Epicurus has been reduced to a tawdry side-show of pleasure-seeking hedonism by many, a place where the Catholic Church desired he remain. Beyond the distain lies a reality Epicurus posited — a nature of things — more closely resembling the findings of modern cosmology than anything else written before the 20th century. Epicurus died in the second century BCE.

The universe, he argued, consists solely of matter and the empty void of space. Matter consists of atoms too tiny to see and of innumerable configurations. When they are in motion changes in their make-up can occur by swerves, or random collisions of atoms. Further, something cannot be made from nothing. In a nutshell that was it, a complete description of reality, the nature of things. William of Oakham would have loved the simplicity of it all.

Following a bit closer, it becomes self-revelatory that there is no god existing invisibly within the universe who both created and may even direct events within it. God is certainly not material. You cannot see or touch God. God cannot be made of the nothingness of empty space. Something cannot be made from nothing. Go down this road and you conclude that there is no inherent point to the universe, no intrinsic meaning or design — and no rewards or punishments after death and no immortal soul. It then becomes obvious that life's object is to seek pleasure and avoid pain — and that's where Epicurus and all his works got stuck with the label of libertine hedonists. Epicurus' idea of pleasure was a temperate one. In his teaching, a good life was attained by adherence to prudence, honor and justice while avoiding delusional pain-inducing desires for the unobtainable. Not unlike the Buddha.

Many centuries later, Epicurus' system served as a foundation for what came to be known as deism – of a divinely rational force, call it god or nature as you choose, that created our universe permeated (on earth at least) by the benevolence, beauty and harmony of its creator. With this job complete, the force forever after does not intervene in the nature of things it has already created. Not unlike Aristotle's Prime Mover or the Big Bang.

All this may be interesting — or deplorable depending on one's beliefs — but what does it have to do with the Declaration of Independence?

A fair amount, actually.

During America's revolutionary era and for a few decades afterward, deism captured the outlook of many of its citizens. In part that is attributable to rejection of the puritanical severity brought ashore at Plymouth Rock, Calvinism's depressing insistence on humankind's utter depravity. Rational people, the Deists knew, were empowered to live honorable and productive lives. Deisms' popularity also reflected the waves of Enlightenment thinking from Europe and Britain that had as an originating precept a powerful strain of anti-clericalism with tendrils running to outright atheism.

Thomas Jefferson was a Deist. His original library, largely assembled by his father, was destroyed by fire in 1770. His later library contained five copies of *On the Nature of Things*, including English, Latin, Italian and French versions. In that library, Jefferson classified religion as a division of moral philosophy. "I consider the genuine (not the reputed) doctrines of Epicurus," the sage of Monticello wrote, "as containing everything rational in moral philosophy which Greece and Rome have left us."

Benjamin Franklin, one of Jefferson's original collaborators in writing the Declaration, was also a Deist. However, he was always careful to reject any contention that that belief made him an atheist. For his part, Jefferson called himself a true Christian, closely studied and wrote about Christ's teachings and considered the Nazarene "the greatest of all reformers."

One of Jefferson's most candid expressions of his beliefs in the realm of moral philosophy came in a letter he wrote to John Adams in 1820, well after his presidency and only a few years before his death. "I feel: therefore, I exist," he wrote. "I feel bodies which are not myself: there are other *existencies* then. I call them *matter*. I feel them changing place. This gives me *motion*. Where there is an absence of matter, I call it *void,* or *nothing*, or *immaterial space.* On the basis of sensation, of matter and motion, we may erect the fabric of all the certainties we can have or need. … When once we quit the basis of sensation all is in the wind. To talk of *immaterial* existences is to talk of *nothings.* To say that the human soul, angels, god, are immaterial, is to say they are *nothings,* or that there is no god, no angels, no soul." Epicurus could have just as well written this extract.

But still, what does this have to do with the Declaration?

The answer is to be found in document's first two and its final paragraphs. These contain the Declaration's four references to — this is actually a bit tricky — a supreme force in the world.

The first reference is to "the laws of nature and of nature's god" in the opening paragraph. Jefferson wrote these words. They are in his handwriting on his original draft now housed in the National Archives. They are an explicit expression of deistic belief — in nature's god — tracing back to Epicurus, and advanced by others in later times, as we shall see.

The second reference is to the second paragraph's assertion that men are endowed with certain rights "by their Creator." This phrase, without the upper-case C later added during congressional consideration, is an edit inserted into Jefferson's draft by Benjamin Franklin. It may easily be read as either deistic or traditionally Christian. It's just the sort of phrase one might expect from Franklin who was always a consensus builder — "We must all hang together or assuredly we shall all hang separately" a comment he made upon signing the Declaration comes to mind.

The final two references are in the final paragraph, being the phrases "the Supreme Judge of the world," and "divine Providence." Both are clearly drawn from the Christian tradition. Both are edits inserted by the Continental Congress.

So, as it turns out, one may find in the Declaration of Independence expressions that are obviously deistic, may be seen as either deistic or Christian, or are obviously Christian.

That is much like how the nation was when the document was written — and not far from how it is today.

None of this is to say Jefferson had a copy of *On the Nature of Things* by his side in writing his first draft. We know he did not. But in seeking the origin and history of the Declaration's principles it is to say that nuances of moral philosophy, personal belief, and traditional Christianity all played important roles.

The last recorded astronomical observation in ancient Greece was made in 475. Prior to that humankind had searched the heavens for both practical and spiritual knowledge since time immemorial. Coinciding roughly with the Roman Empire's collapse, that stopped and was not resumed in the West for a thousand years.

For that millennia the Western mind was isolated within a hard crust of orthodox dogma that made even the idea of curiosity heretical. Of course, there were exceptions. Among them, as we have seen, was Thomas Aquinas' attempt to reconcile faith with reason. The dominant paradigm, however, outside the realms of trade and war where reason did rule, was obedience to the revealed word of God as proclaimed by the Catholic Church.

That crust was split wide open by the Scientific Revolution that ran from the time of Copernicus to Newton's description of gravity a hundred and fifty years later. Not only did curiosity about the heavens and the material world pour through the cracks, but so too did curiosity about humankind's rightful relationship with itself. The outpouring released after an epoch of suppression produced a profusion of creative thought that we now look upon as the Enlightenment.

There's more than one step to getting there, however, and we'll start briefly at the beginning, with Genesis.

God created Earth and set the heavens above it. He created all the fishes, birds, animals, and creeping things. He then created man and woman and set them to subdue and rule over the Earth. So read the opening lines of the Hebrew Book of Genesis.

The image resembles a hollow glass sphere containing our planet and all the rest with the stars sprinkled about the outer surface. God presumably could hold that sphere in his hands, observe it and all that occurred within it. Such, at least, is one approximate description of what the universe looked like to those living in the West 800 years ago and for roughly 800 years before that. The universe was everything that could be seen from Earth up to the outer most sphere of stars. Set that worldview in your mind and the utter supremacy of God and the complete submission of humankind to his will is manifest. If you start to break that sphere up, you're breaking up the entire order of things.

A hundred or so years before Genesis was written, the Greek astronomer Aristarchus posited that the sun was located at the center of the then-observable planetary system with the Earth not only orbiting around it but making one full rotation on its axis daily. The rotation accounted for the appearance of the sun seeming to rise in the east and set in the west. That idea did not withstand either Plato or Aristotle.

Plato, as we've noted, was the philosopher of perfect Forms. Since the circle is the perfect expression of a Form, he reasoned, and nature is an expression of perfection, it follows that planetary orbits must be perfect circles and that all motion within those circles must be at a uniform speed. His version of perfection placed the Earth at the center of it all. The sun orbited Earth, not the other way around. The gods of Babylon and Egypt perpetually riding golden barges or chariots through the sky from the darkness to the light were supplanted by perfection.

Though he rejected much else from his teacher, Aristotle adopted Plato's scheme of perfectly circular planetary motions centered on a static Earth at the center. He even envisioned a model requiring fifty-four circles within circles to account for the motion of the sun and five planets that can be seen with the naked eye. This profusion of circles was necessary to account for the observable non-circular planetary motions, especially the elongated ellipse followed by Mars. The idea of perfection simply overwhelmed any messy concepts contrary to it.

Aristotle's Earth-centered system of perfect circles hardened into orthodox truth, especially as scholasticism based on his teachings tightened its grip on the Western mind. There is a special irony here in that Aristotle was also the voice of reasoned deduction based upon examination of available evidence. It is history's premier case of a centuries-long intellectual statis based on accepting the teacher's conclusion, not on how he or she teaches us to reach conclusions on our own.

Some 400 years later the Egyptian savant Ptolemy of Alexandria came up with a Ferris wheel-like contraption of forty wheels to perfect the perfect circles model. The primary wheel had secondary wheels, some running clockwise, some counterclockwise, whose motions rendered various shapes from ovals to ellipses and even backward progression. Spinning the whole thing up, with the Earth placed slightly off center, created a plausible replica of Aristotle's universe.

Plausible was good enough for fourteen centuries.

The Earth centered system suited the era due in part to its provenance back to the intellectual icons of ancient Greece and in part due to unchallenged mental inertia. It also fit nicely with Biblical reference. The Genesis story implies it. A verse in Psalms had God establishing the Earth "So that it shall never be moved." We find in Joshua that "the sun stood still, and the moon stopped." These and similar excerpts hardly constitute the foundations of faith but they are markers in a text held to be the word of God.

More than quibbling over a few scriptural verses was at stake. So too was the concept of humankind being at the center of creation as affirmed by God's word. Knock the Earth out of the center and humankind perforce goes with it.

The Scientific Revolution unfolded over nearly a century and a half, beginning in 1543 with the publication of

Nicholas Copernicus' thesis that the Earth and other planets orbit the sun in perfect circles. He was shown the first manuscript pages on his deathbed, having delayed bringing his astronomical findings to print at least in part to avoid the controversy he thought would ensue. As it turned out, his work only provoked mild remonstrance on religious grounds and was soon circulating in academic circles and even taught in courses on cosmology.

A half-century later Johannes Kepler began the publication of a series of works that constitute the foundation for the modern understanding of our solar system. The sun, he wrote, was not the center of the system, but rather the focal point of a series of ellipses that described the orbits of Earth and the other planets around it. Based on observations and his own calculation, he noted that in elliptical orbits planets moved faster when they were closer to the sun and slower when they were farther away. In an enticing phrase, he held that God wanted humankind, created in his image, to recognize the physical laws that governed the system "so that we could share his own thoughts."

In the same period during which Kepler worked, the Italian astronomer Galileo Galilei, using a telescope made by Kepler, discovered three of the large moons that orbit Saturn. This was not supposed to be. Aristotelian cosmology only allowed planetary objects to orbit Earth. Galileo stepped into the briar patch, however, not due to his own work but simply because he wrote that he agreed with Copernicus' close-to-sun-centered system. A huge public controversy followed as the Catholic Church turned the floodlights on to what it wanted to be kept in the dark. Upon investigation the church Inquisition found that the idea the sun is the "center of the World" was "foolish and absurd, philosophically and formally heretical inasmuch as it expressly contradicts the doctrine of the Holy Scripture." Galileo was ordered to renounce his heretical views and sentenced to house arrest. In the meantime, other astronomers published confirmations of Galileo's observations.

Finally, sweeping the scholastic cosmological system into the dustbin, Isaac Newton published his *Principia* in 1687, the theory of gravity that explains why Kepler's planetary objects follow their orbits instead of falling out of the sky.

The power of these discoveries went far beyond the subjects they examined. They were not mere opinions challenging orthodoxy. They were the product of reason without reference to revelation. They opened a unique gateway giving humankind potentially illimitable access to understanding. How might a society based upon reason look? How might a government based on reason operate? It was a whole new world.

Thomas Hobbes.
Portrait by John
Michael Wright.

Source: Wikimedia

Baruch Spinoza.
Anonymous portrait.

Source: Wikipedia

Hobbes & Spinoza

Imagine with me for a moment, if you will, what it would be like once again for the first time to sense the liberating realization that no dogmas of the past ruled the pages of freedom that might be written in the future. Clear the stage of all the old props and the script of every conforming trope. Start anew.

To grasp that exhilaration is to gain an insight into the feelings alive among those who created what we now know as the age of European Enlightenment. Many of the era's thinkers, poets, wits and scholars — those who played with fire — lived at least partially sub rosa lives, in exile or hiding, a step ahead of the king's jailors and the pope's censors, their public persona at times concealing more provocative private beliefs.

Once you have swept the stage clear, what do you do then? How do you rebuild society, at least in your mind, after you have cast its predecessors aside? For some, that meant going back to the root of the matter, to an imaginary time before time. Discourse on an individual's place in a state of nature, a hypothetical epoch before law and rulers, became popular. So too did variations on the oldest theme of human cooperation, the ancient Hebrew admonition to do unto others as you would have them do unto you. The paradigm is elegant. Reduce all associations to their most primitive beginnings, then be guided in creating a rational social contract by reciprocal pledges to avoid being abused by others by not abusing them. Refine the concept to an individual plane and consignment to predetermined ruts in life can give way to ideas like liberty, inalienable rights, and unrestrained inquisitiveness.

The Englishman Thomas Hobbes was among the first to develop this line of thinking. Some credit him with writing the opening chapter of modern political philosophy in his major work *Leviathan* published in 1651. Hobbes scrapped the theory of governance based on the duties subjects owed to king or prelate. He posited instead a body of reserved rights citizens retain in a social contract creating an authority to enforce powers delegated to it by the citizenry. In his model natural rights derived from reason replace moral and political principles based on Scripture. Humankind was free to navigate its own political future without dependence on any version of divine direction.

Interestingly, Hobbes acknowledged that all his precepts of moral conduct could be found in the Bible. Their authority, however, hinged on their being embedded in reason rather than occurrence in the Book of Deuteronomy or a letter written to Roman Christians in the time of Nero. Hobbes' moral precepts are his rendering of the sum of human experience, acknowledged across diverse cultures and readily understood as common sense. For his efforts, Hobbes was denounced as a heretic and atheist, deeply corrosive charges he publicly denied. His works were burned on the Oxford University quad. He fled England for exile in France to avoid disfavor, then later fled back to England to escape possible harm from other English royalists in exile there. He died in 1679 at the age of ninety-one.

Hobbes' dour view of humankind led him to a deeply conservative answer to the question of governance. The state of nature he envisioned was of every individual at perpetual war with every other individual. Human passions were the motive force behind an insatiable drive to amass power in incremental steps toward the unobtainable goal of full protection against attack and possible death. In this condition, the boulder was always and only being pushed up the hill. "Continual feare, and danger of violent death" dominated the state of nature, he believed, leaving "the life of man solitary, poore, brutish, nasty and short."

Augustine would have understood. Hardly a jumping off point for a leap into the exhilarating possibilities of democratic self-rule. Hobbes scorned democracy. Early in his writing career, he had translated the Latin text of Thucydides' *The Peloponnesian War* into English. His disdain for democratic rule may have been fostered by the work's repeated examples of democracies led astray by internal faction and dissent or by whims of popular passion and demagogic misguidance.

A short aside is warranted to note that while Hobbes is not credited with a particular influence on the Declaration, his view of humanity was shared by many who drafted the Constitution more than a decade later. The passionate pursuit of personal interest was not alien to them. In crafting an organic law for representative democracy, accounting for that passion meant checking power with power, balancing the interests of one group against those of another, and giving the minority a path to avoid being easily overwhelmed by the majority. Hobbes did not believe in the perfectibility of humankind as did some other Enlightenment thinkers. The framers were largely of a similar bent. Accomplishing anything major under the Constitution was made deliberately difficult as a guard against precipitate action.

Hobbes did not deny that in transitioning from a state of nature groups of people might choose democracy, he just disparaged it. Monarchy was his choice: unitary rule capable of acting swiftly to danger. The ruler's obligation was to protect society against war, anarchy, and instability — a slide back into the terrors of the state of nature. Almost as an afterthought, he granted that the ruler should govern in accordance with the compact drawn up by those who are governed. He also argued that when "our refusal to obey frustrates the end for which the sovereignty was ordained, then there is no liberty to refuse; otherwise, there is." That "otherwise there is" was Hobbes' reluctant consent to a right to revolt. The truth is he hated the idea, believing it far better to suffer a ruler's occasional abuses than to risk chaos in overturning authority however abusive. At bottom, Hobbes left out the part that others later insisted upon: provision making the ruler accountable to those being ruled.

From this point forward, however, the conservative Hobbes drafts a new covenant in which one can discern the outlines of this nation's founding principles.

The first right of liberty is the right to self-preservation, to self-defense. It applies equally to all. William of Ockham understood this. Call it a right to life. To assure life, Hobbes believed, reason dictates humankind follow "the first, and Fundamental Law of Nature … to seek Peace, and follow it." The perpetual war imposed by a state of nature — the very contradiction of a right to life — can best be avoided by a compact among those who otherwise would be set against one another. The compact must be voluntary. Agreement to it flows from the act of adopting it, or by acting in accordance with it once it is in place. The compact represents the will of the people so that the ruler expresses their will in abiding by it. Hobbes knew that virtually all governments up to his time were based on an originating act of conquest or coercion. He was envisioning a whole new world.

Adopting a compact was an act of surrendering untrammeled liberty for sufficient security to ensure self-preservation. In Hobbes' view "men should divest themselves of their right to do all things … so that a man be willing, when others are so too … to lay down [his] right to all things and be contented with so much liberty against other men as he would allow other men against himself."

The liberty surrendered, of course, are those rights to act that are invested in the governing authority, in a monarch according to Hobbes' preference. Rights not surrendered are retained. In this design, people only lose what they voluntarily give away for the sake of peace.

Further in Hobbes' view "as long as men arrogate to themselves more honor than they give to others, it cannot be imagined how they can possibly live in peace: and consequently, we are to suppose, that for peace's sake, nature hath ordained this law, *that every man acknowledge [every] other for his equal.*" More directly he wrote "we are by nature equal, not unequal, that there is no natural aristocracy, no natural division into workers and rulers, and that all political hierarchy is a contrivance."

All Hobbes' structure is predicated upon reason, and the natural laws and natural rights derived from it. The principle of universal equality can be found in Scripture, as in Paul's writing to Galatians (3:28) that all are one in Christ, there being no distinction between Jew and Greek, or bonded and free. The crucial difference is that no supernatural force need be invoked to validate Hobbes' construct. Reason alone does that, reason inherent in human nature, reason as a human possession rather than some encrypted code impressed on the minds of humans by God.

Hobbes' entire theory can be expressed most simply in a turn on a phrase that predates Scripture: Do not unto others what you would not have them do unto you — restrain your own liberty to act according to the same restraint others show to you. Humankind's seeking peace from an initial condition of war and its articulation of natural laws that give rise to natural rights, lead inexorably to the humble admonition to treat your neighbor as you would have your neighbor treat you. Something approaching the level of awe is involved in reaching into prehistory and extracting this most basic and ancient understanding from it as the foundation for modern society.

Hobbes enumerated twenty-one natural laws, immutable distillations of human experience that are more prosaic than majestic. Keep your word. Get along with others. Acknowledge the natural equality of others with you. His concept of liberty carries more heft the more you examine it. In the state of nature liberty of action is the direct legacy of being alive. It is neither granted from above nor earned piecemeal. Liberty is humanity's pre-political endowment. In respect to individual freedom, liberty is also inalienable. No person can, with moral correctness, surrender liberty for slavery. Nor can any person in accordance with natural law or rights arbitrarily trade life for death. The inalienable attributes of life and liberty are the prerequisites by which each individual may pursue what they see as their best interests, an inalienable right to the pursuit of happiness, if you will.

Certain rights inherent to liberty may be restrained or delegated by the terms of the social compact, such as rights to property or to declare war or print money. The great residual remains with the individual: to speak, to write, to gather together, to acquire and divest, to inquire, to create, to stand Yea or Nay on any public proposition. These are the jewels of public life granted by liberty. In Hobbes' view, they are yours by virtue of your humanity. Regulation, law, custom and tradition may affect them, but they do not create them.

This may all seem idealistic or even naïve, but upon such beliefs Western humanity has drawn an arc of freedom around the individual to replace the bondage of a fate determined before birth.

I will note as an aside that has been mentioned previously and will be addressed later that natural laws and rights in the 21st century have all the powers that any other set of words have: none by themselves. Today enforceable rights can be found in positive law, regulation and legal contract. Many people today no doubt believe that the right to free speech or freedom of religion are not only protected by but originate in and are granted by the Constitution's First Amendment. The idea that they preexist that or any other document has largely been washed out of our consciousness. The difference is not trifling. Rights that are given can be taken away. Natural rights are immutable. Let's note too that Hobbes' perpetual war state of nature is purely his own hypothetical. Aristotle held that humankind is predisposed to political association. John Locke, another English philosopher who we will soon encounter, did too when he hypothesized his version of a state of nature.

Before moving on from Hobbes let us take a moment to unpack what he taught compared to the principles expressed in the Declaration of Independence. Hobbes did not inject a creator into his work, either deistic or divine. None was necessary. Crucially for Hobbes his model relied only on humans working out natural laws and rights for themselves without intervention of any kind. The Declaration's opening invocation of the Laws of Nature certainly echoes Hobbes. The phrase "We hold these truths to be self-evident" is clearly not directly from his work. The stretch, however, between Hobbes immutable natural laws and rights and the Declaration's self-evident truths is a distinction without a significant difference. If one permits a link between pursuing one's self-interest and the pursuit of happiness, then an additional similarity between Hobbes and the Declaration exists. The Declaration's "governments are instituted among men" carries the same revolutionary message of self-government as does Hobbes' social compact — in both cases humans of and by themselves are deemed capable of creating their own government.

By way of illustration, reciting the Declaration's principles using bold italics for parallels with Hobbes, regular italics for similarities, and normal type for the remainder, the result is: *"We hold these truths to be self-evident,* ***that all men are created equal and that they are endowed*** by their Creator ***with certain inalienable rights, that among these are life,*** *liberty and the pursuit of happiness.* ***That to ensure these rights, Governments are instituted among Men, deriving their just powers from the consent of the governed."***

On February 17, 1600, normal business was halted at a popular marketplace in central Rome. The pause was to let justice be done. After a seven-year trial during which he was imprisoned, the sentence rendered against philosopher Giordano Bruno was carried out. He had publicly held God and Nature to be one. The Inquisition court that heard his case also discovered other heresies from his writings, including denying that the mother of Christ was a virgin. Bruno had refused to recant. He was stripped naked, nailed upside down on a cross with a gag in his mouth and burned alive.

In 1677 another philosopher died in more peaceful circumstances in the Hague. The first of Baruch Spinoza's major works, *Ethics*, was published after his death, delaying the criticism he knew would follow. An earlier volume, *Theological-Political Treatise*, had come out listing an anonymous author, falsely citing Hamburg as the city of publication, and printed in Latin to limit its exposure to the well-educated. As a young man Spinoza's beliefs got him expelled from his synagogue. He lived modestly, usually in some small village outside a major city, confining his views and his writing to a close circle of friends, making his way by grinding lenses for telescopes and microscopes. He died at the age of forty-four from lung inflammation possibly caused by inhaling tiny glass fibers. Holland banned his works. So did Rome. His alleged crime was the worst of blasphemes, the denial of God, atheism.

Jesus purportedly said "The truth shall set your free." Spinoza would have agreed, with the caveat that the only path to truth is reason. A "free man," Spinoza held, is "one who lives according to the dictates of reason alone." This austere discipline led Spinoza to the further conclusion that all religion is no more than "organized superstition."

Spinoza has much in common with Epicurus, although his knowledge of the Greek philosopher lies in the realm of speculation. Both believed that the universe is composed of but a single substance that presents itself in an infinity of forms. God is simply the expression of nature's capacity to reveal matter in all its potential for life, beauty, and physical reality of every kind. God is the impulse for infinite expression in nature, its living dynamic. God is the motive power of Nature. God and nature are inseparably one. God is Nature.

Albert Einstein understood this concept having once said "I am not an atheist. ... I believe in Spinoza's God who reveals himself in the orderly harmony of what exists, not in a God who concerns himself with fates and actions of human beings." Jefferson, whose library contained works by Spinoza and Epicurus, held a similar view, marked by his phrase "Nature's God" in the Declaration's first sentence.

From at least Aquinas' era, an intellectual struggle over the roles of religion and reason challenged the Western mind. Could the two be reconciled? Did God implant in the human mind templates for natural laws that humans later discovered within themselves using right reason? For a century up to the 1750s Spinoza commanded the most radical ground in challenging everything from revealed religion to divinely sanctioned authority.

Design and purpose define Christianity. God designed Earth for humans. Salvation is the purpose of life. All the rest is residue. This cosmology existed within God's mind before any of it was made real. Life is no more than a reflection of God's will. When a purpose is declared, means to enforce it must be created. Thus, the church's role in regulating, overseeing, and teaching all that is required to justify dogma and doctrine. The struggle for salvation engenders a surety of rewards and punishments in a life after life along with a complex nomenclature of control, a mindset of obedience, a necessity to conform and in the process creation of a hierarchy of rule, status, and differentiation between those deserving blessings and those deserving damnation.

Spinoza rewrote cosmology. He did not take God out of the equation. He reimagined God as the motive force nature displays rather than an omnipotent being existing separate and apart from it. Nature is perfect in following immutable laws of cause and effect. Reason gives humans the capacity to test theories attempting to explain these laws. Nature has neither design nor purpose and is indifferent to whatever it does create. "Nature has no end set before it," Spinoza believed, and "all final causes are nothing but human fictions." To alter or interrupt nature's course would violate nature's perfection. Christianity's God can, as it were, stand outside of nature and on occasion reach into its fabric to make it do something contrary to itself. Bringing the dead back to life, for example. Because Spinoza's God is Nature, Nature would be ungodly if it acted against its own laws. Nature cannot act contrary to itself. Miracles do not exist. Spinoza maintained that in a world ruled by reason, "miracles and ignorance are the same."

Comprehending Spinoza's argument is not difficult. Accepting it can be world shattering. Life's great stage is barer and more austere when Spinoza's logic is applied to it. All that stuff you can't see, that's because it isn't there. Gone is the long-bearded God dispensing wrath or mercy according to his unknowable will. Gone too is the divinity of Christ, but not the preacher who counseled love in the face of an imminent apocalypse. There are no demons, or Devil, or evil spirits. Angels disappear, including guardian angels. No spirit guards a river or a lake. Apparitions are mere chimera. The body has no soul. No life awaits after death. Superstition's props are the creations of a confused imagination. Prayers to save an ill child are heard only by the supplicant. Neither Heaven nor Hell exist. No one is destined to greatness or to failure. There is no destiny.

All that is left on the stage are humans free to direct their lives as they see fit. Sentiments like these kept Spinoza under surveillance for much of his life. Several of his similarly-minded associates were imprisoned for their views. A few were executed. Many were forced into clandestine lives, living like spies in a foreign land.

Spinoza is best known for his views on revealed religion. His mark also shows in politics and governance. The modern understanding of what freedom of thought is Spinoza. In one of the earliest historical references to inalienable rights, Spinoza maintained that "everyone has an inalienable right over his thoughts." Governments may try to control opinion, and cardinals may try to define conscience, but Spinoza argued "no one can willingly transfer his natural right of free reason and judgment, or be compelled to do so." Spinoza defied the common wisdom of his age that ordinary people had to be instructed by their betters about what was right or wrong, true or false.

To have meaning, the rights of conscience require a protective cordon of societal tolerance. That tolerance, Spinoza believed, had to extend to contrary and dissenting views, although it did not, in his view, embrace sedition. Its spirit is best captured in the phrase said to reflect the belief of the Enlightenment savant Voltaire that "I may disapprove of what you say, but I will defend to the death your right to say it." In Spinoza's time, debates over tolerance centered on whether Protestants (or Catholics) should tolerate coexistence with Catholics (or Protestants). In a later era, Jefferson treasured drafting a Virginia law of religious toleration among his greatest achievements in life.

Spinoza shared Hobbes' view that people formed social compacts as a flight to safety. From there they parted ways. As we have seen, Hobbes distrusted the public's susceptibility to guile and faction, insisting that a monarch should be invested with absolute authority. In Spinoza's view, liberty is the point of government, its object being to enable individuals "to develop their minds and bodies in security, and to employ their reason unshackled." He believed democracy most closely approximates the freedoms which "Nature grants to all. One can consult and participate. ... In this way all men remain equal as they were before in the state of Nature." The Declaration conveys Spinoza's view of the equality of all men and their endowment with certain unalienable rights. Neither the document nor the man included women in their formulation.

In a fitting irony, Elizabeth Cady Stanton and her colleagues who organized the seminal 1844 Seneca Convention in New York on women's rights used the Declaration as their template in asserting their own claim to equality. Since its adoption, the rite of passage to full citizenship in this country rests upon being taken under the Declaration's wing.

John Locke, above, in portrait by Godfrey Kneller, and Algernon Sydney as a young man by unknown artist.

Source: Wikimedia.

Enlightenment

"Long is the way, and hard, that out of hell leads up to the light," is the poet John Milton's one-sentence version of this essay's entire narrative.

The light, of course, is the Enlightenment, a space in time from the 17th century to the French Revolution during which Western individualism took form in the articulation of liberal democracy. That broad picture is composed of different Enlightenments, radical and moderate arising in different regions including French salons, English clubs and taverns, Scottish universities, safe havens for exiles scattered from the Netherlands to Geneva, and somewhat later in Germany.

The whole enterprise aimed on one hand at disenthralling humanity from reliance on religion to define governance and on the other to place governance in the hands of the individuals to be governed.

For our purposes it is useful to focus on that portion of the Enlightenment that most influenced Thomas Jefferson and his American revolutionary compatriots. The events that molded Jefferson's political beliefs prior to the American Revolution occurred before he was born in 1743. This is not the least unusual. Think of those born after World War II who played out their most productive years in the bipolar world of nuclear-armed superpowers that emerged after the war. For Jefferson, the pivotal event was England's Glorious Revolution of 1688 and its consequences. This revolution sowed the seed for the Anglophile Toryism of those like America's Alexander Hamilton and the decidedly Whiggish bent of Jefferson and others that created an American divide between alignments with Britain or with France that played out well past Jefferson's term in the White House that ended in 1809.

The Glorious Revolution had its antecedents in the beheading of King Charles I in 1649. Charles demonstrated his conviction in his divine right to rule by imposing taxes without seeking parliamentary consent. His marriage to a Roman Catholic aroused fear of his papal sympathies. The upshot was that he lost his head while England lost its freedom in Lord Protector Oliver Cromwell's democracy turned tyranny. Once Cromwellian rule was swept aside, Protestant King Charles II was crowned in 1660.

Algernon Sydney was among those dissatisfied with the dynasty's restoration.

Hollywood could hardly top his life story. Sydney was born an aristocrat in 1623, suffered severe wounds as a colonel leading a calvary charge against the then-king's army, served as a commissioner at the trial of King Charles I that resulted in his beheading, was later forced to flee to Europe when Charles II assumed the throne, shuffled about the continent for twenty years "as a vagabond … forsaken by my friends," twice evaded assassination by royal agents, and was given permission to return to England in 1677. That's when the historically important part of his life began, as we will soon see.

James II brought his forebearers' belief in absolute monarchy with him. He was also Catholic. Some dissenters like Sydney feared, correctly as it turned out, that James conspired with France's King Louis XIV, to bring centralized rule and the Catholic religion to England.

Dissenters' trust in the monarchy is reflected in Sydney's remark that "To depend upon the Will of a Man is Slavery." He engaged in a fierce debate with one of the king's chief propagandists who argued both for the divine right to rule and the right of absolute rule. During this period, Sydney wrote his major work *Discourses Concerning Government* which was not published until fifteen years after its author died. This is the book that drew Jefferson's attention several decades later. In it Sydney makes what are now considered classic cases for the freedom of all individuals and their collective right to form a social contract reflecting their sovereign decisions on governance. In the summer of 1683, he was arrested for plotting to murder the king and was executed before the year was out.

John Locke was another prominent English dissenter who lived in clandestine exile for years, assuming the names Dr. van den Linden or Dr. Lynne to hide his identity. One admirer credited him with works "by which the very soul of despotism in Great Britain had received its death wound."

Maybe, and that's the point.

The Glorious Revolution saw the ascension of Protestant King William III, fixed a firm foundation for Parliamentary rule and brought in its wake both a Declaration of Rights and a Toleration Act that expanded freedom of worship for some, but by no means all, unorthodox believers. The revolution fixed the principle that the law stood above the prince, making the people the ultimate source of sovereignty, a tectonic shift away from the divine right of kings. What was glorious to some, however, was betrayal to others. The revolution saw England's landed aristocracy sink its talons into a grip on power that lasted for two centuries until the Empire unraveled.

What stung Jefferson most decades into the new dynasty was a profound sense of opportunity squandered. The king was surrounded by a standing army. The new Bank of England bought off members of Parliament and anyone else who needed persuasion. Ministerial government usurped separation of powers. Parliament was corrupted by members owing their pensions or military rank to the crown. Many in that body owed their first loyalty to the king, his court and his ministers. Two years before America's Declaration of Independence, the English writer James Burgh concluded that his country had become "a licensed tyranny instead of a free government."

This history, as well as all the Enlightenment inspiration from England and elsewhere, is what steeled Jefferson to his task, along with his more radical aspirants to freedom and their more moderate brethren to break with the mother country by founding a republic.

John Locke and Baruch Spinoza were born in 1632 and became respectively archetypes of moderate and radical enlightenment thinking. Locke was the product of his times, a struggle against the threat of monarchial tyranny intensified by religious fractures. Spinoza was a product of his mind, a search for truth while living at society's margin.

Locke believed the people were free to choose their own form of government and accepted constitutional monarchy. Spinoza believed democracy in some form was essential to liberty, although he had deep concerns about mass passions and uninformed democracy.

A Calvinist, Locke supported the Toleration Act that excluded non-believers, Catholics, Jews, Quakers and Deists and all who denied the Trinity. Spinoza set no limits on the boundaries of freedom of conscience and freedom of thought. Locke believed that together with reason the divine design in nature provided a path to truth. Spinoza posited reason as the only path to truth. Locke urged that humanity's God-given faculty of reason be used to discover the principles of living and governing. Spinoza set out to free humanity of the fetters of religion and superstition altogether. Locke's God can be found in Scripture. Spinoza's God is the creative force of Nature itself. Their era has been described as "the first great manifestation of the modern revolutionary temper."

The two traditions produced similar sets of political consensuses that the people are sovereign, that legitimacy requires consent of the governed, and that all are born equal with certain fundamental natural rights. Locke and Algernon Sidney were the best-known proponents throughout Europe and America of a moderate path to revolutionary change because they were the voices of that change in the most riveting political event of their times, the Glorious Revolution. Jefferson cited the influence of both of them in writing the Declaration. The French wit and skewer of clerical and social hypocrisy Voltaire wrote in the moderate tradition. In one of his more scathing observations, he asked why a benevolent God condemned Adam and every generation after him "for having swallowed an apple?" Another moderate, Voltaire's fellow-countryman Montesquieu anonymously published his *Spirit of the Laws* that was familiar to those in America who drafted the Declaration and the Constitution. Radical enlightenment thinkers like Spinoza are more often found in the spectrum between deism and non-belief. They were known in revolutionary America but were less influential than their moderate brethren. The radicals include the French founder of the *Encyclopédie* Denis Diderot, his companion Baron d' Holbach, who twice weekly turned his Paris home into a grand salon, and the aloof, skittish and brilliant Jean-Jacques Rousseau who opened the door to romanticism that did not go down well among Calvinist and Presbyterian Americans. The Scots also made major contributions including those by Francis Hutcheson who was the chair of moral philosophy at Glasgow University for seventeen years and his one-time student the conservative David Hume who had no appetite for revealed religion at all.

John Locke served the interests of England's landed gentry so it is little wonder that his most famous formulation of political rights is the trinity of "life, liberty and property." Property had a board meaning for Locke. Encompassing not just assets that might be bought or sold, Locke's property included one's person, life, liberty, and estate. Property was the sum of all possessions. Historians still debate whether the Founding Fathers were more interested in protecting their alienable property — that at the time included Black slaves heavily weighted the farther South one went — or their and their countrymen's liberty. Even up to the Civil War anti-slavery leaders including Abraham Lincoln claimed no Constitutional basis for doing anything about slavery in states where it already existed. Jefferson himself lived in seignorial elegance while disparaging the debasement of Blacks who made the elegance possible. The Founders struck an ends justifies the means compromise that served both their purposes. Jefferson lived with his own contradictions and a palpable dread of the price that was sure to come due for abiding slavery. We do not know why Jefferson chose the "pursuit of happiness" in writing the Declaration over the Lockian variant of "life, liberty and property." Perhaps he wanted to avoid an endorsement of slavery in setting out the self-evident truths by which the new nation entered the world. Perhaps he simply believed the term "happiness" was more felicitous or bold. At all events, his choice was a good one.

To be sure, Locke had no grudge against happiness. In *Concerning Human Understanding* he wrote "The necessity of pursuing happiness [is] the foundation of liberty." David Hume's contrarian view expressed decades later was that "happiness is not to be dreamed of" as an object of government. But that was hard-minded David Hume. As we have seen, one can go back at least as far as the ancient Greek philosophers for assertions that happiness, rightly understood, is the object of life. Francis Hutcheson, among the most widely read Enlightenment writers in America prior to the revolution coined the phrase that "that action is best, which procures the greatest happiness for the greatest number."

As Jefferson noted, the Declaration's principles express the language and political discourse common to his time. One did not need to open a textbook to know that colonists groused that instead of taxing without representation, the British government should foster their inalienable natural rights to such aims as the possession of property and the pursuit of happiness. A prime example is a document Jefferson acknowledged he had available when he was drafting the Declaration. Less than a month earlier George Mason had helped write the Virginia Declaration of Rights. It captures perfectly the gusts of revolutionary thinking that Jefferson rendered into the Declaration's eloquence. It declared "that all men are created equally free and independent, and have certain inherent natural Rights, of which they cannot, by any Compact, deprive or divest their posterity; among which are the Enjoyment of Life and Liberty, with the Means of acquiring and possessing property, and pursuing and obtaining Happiness and Safety." By comparison, the parallel portion of Jefferson's first draft reads "that all men are created equal and independent (sic), that from that equal creation they derive rights inherent and inalienable, among which are the preservation of life, and liberty, and the pursuit of happiness." One can find in both documents' traces of the Stoics, Cicero, Aquinas, Oakham, Erasmus, Luther, Hobbes, Spinoza, Locke, Sidney, Hutcheson and many others who risked their freedom and their lives to contribute to the self-evident truths shared by Jefferson and his peers. In a sense, it is silly to claim Jefferson must have picked this-or-that phrase from this-or-that philosopher when he could pluck them out of the air in the intensifying swirl of revolutionary rhetoric surrounding him.

The term "pursuit of happiness" deserves a word more. See it as the culmination of the struggle over the purpose of government since the fall of Rome. In context that pursuit rests on such inalienable rights as life and liberty based on government by consent of the governed. In its final measure, pursuit of happiness always comes down to an attribute of a single individual. From the individual's being in some capacity the ruling authority's supplicant or servant, to having government be the individual's servant is the conceptual territory over which Western humanity fought for roughly 1,200 years. Just as the Declaration is a capstone to that struggle, the pursuit of happiness expresses the individual's primacy in the whole endeavor.

One should not lose sight of such things.

In his major work *Two Treatises of Government* Locke did not use the term "inalienable rights," but he came close. He evoked the term an "appeal to Heaven" in justifying a right to revolution that resides with the people "by a law antecedent and paramount to all positive laws of men." The lineage to the right to revolt against unjust rule dates at least as far back as Oakham. If one sees the individual from Locke's perspective as not only the person, but that person's life, liberty, and estates then rights to revolution and self-preservation are closely linked. A rulers' wide-scale abuse of personal liberty or property is equally an assault on the individual, justifying revolution by society and invoking the right to self-preservation by individuals.

Francis Hutcheson's view was similar. "For whenever any invasion is made upon unalienable Rights, there must arise," he wrote, "a ... Right to Resistance. ... Unalienable Rights are essential Limitations in all Governments." George Mason's Virginia Declaration also ties unalienable rights to a right to resist. A "Majority of the Community," it states, when faced with a government's failure to meet its obligations to the people "hath an indubitable, unalienable, and indefeasible Right, to reform, alter, or abolish it ...." These sentiments found their way into the Declaration as "whenever any form of government becomes destructive of these ends, it is the right of the people to alter or to abolish it, and to institute new government, laying its foundation on such principles, and organizing its powers in such form, as to them shall seem most likely to affect their safety and happiness."

Jefferson's touch to all this was to enumerate the three inalienable rights that best protected the individual's place in society — rights to life, liberty and the pursuit of happiness. He did so by counting them as "among those" that individuals are endowed with by their creator. The list is deliberately indefinite. The intent is to allow for the expansion of individual rights, not their limitation. Jefferson concurred with Spinoza's classifying freedom of thought and conscience as inalienable. The Constitution's first amendment confirms this belief among the members of Congress who adopted it. The Bill of Rights flows naturally from the Declaration's principles and, like the Declaration, is deliberately indefinite with the Tenth Amendment's reference to "The powers not delegated to the United States by the Constitution, nor prohibited by it to the States, are reserved to the States respectively, or to the people." This structure invites inclusion. People of color and all women know this story.

As to inalienable rights, the term is most often rendered to mean a right that the individual cannot morally transfer to the state or anywhere else. All inalienable rights derive from natural human rights, but not all natural rights are inalienable. One may have a natural right to drink water from the well, but that right may be transferred. No person may rightfully surrender their right of conscience to another.

One word not found in the Declaration that was a staple of Enlightenment thinking is 'democracy.' A theme pre-dating the Enlightenment that finds a secure place in the Declaration is the sovereignty of the people. The document declares its announcement of independence is made "in the Name, and by Authority of the good People" of the united colonies. But it is silent on the type of government

independence will bring — that clearly was not known until the draft Constitution was ratified — except to note that governments derive "their just Powers from the Consent of the Governed." As everyone knew, the Glorious Revolution created a government based on common consent that gave place to king, commons and the aristocracy. When it came time to draft the Constitution, the Founders were constrained in making room for democracy. Alexander Hamilton, a New York delegate to the Constitutional Convention, thought democracy could too easily lead to mob rule. "The people do not want virtue," declared his Bay State colleague Elbridge Gerry. They "are the dupes of pretended patriots." Connecticut's Roger Sherman believed the people "should have as little to do as may be about the government." The president was to be chosen by a set of electors bypassing direct popular election. State legislatures were to elect senators. Only representatives were elected directly by the people, meaning only white men, and often only white men owning property, with enslaved Blacks to be counted as three-fifths of a human being. The result was our federated Republic, a representative democracy of united states.

All this certainly would have been going too far for David Hume. He liked Britain's mixed government best, thought democracy "too turbulent" and considered the idea of rule by consent of the governed ridiculous. Historically, Hume pointed out, governments were based on force. The American experiment truly was to be something new.

Obtaining the consent of the governed is easy enough to imagine when forming a new government. How later generations grant that consent once a government is formed was mostly glossed over by Enlightenment writers. Locke did address the subject, however, writing that to retain legitimacy each succeeding generation needs to register its consent to the original compact. In practical terms, voting and accepting the result provides the grant of consent linking every citizen directly to events in 1776 and 1789.

Historiography is dense with citation and analysis of word traces found in the works of some Enlightenment thinkers that appear verbatim in the Declaration. Was Jefferson copying Locke when he wrote of "a long chain of abuses" by the British king? Or when Locke's words "are more disposed to suffer" appear in the Declaration? Did he recall these words from reading Locke, or were they common political currency of his era, sometimes attributed to John Locke and sometimes not? The same type of question can be asked about phrases that first appear in Francis Hutcheson's works that also turn up in the Declaration. Once again, while Jefferson acknowledged an intellectual debt to Locke, Sidney and others dating back to Aristotle and Cicero, his own testimony is that he did not copy "from any particular and previous writing" in drafting the Declaration that was "was intended to be an expression of the American mind." All its authority, he wrote, rested on "the harmonizing sentiments of the day, whether expressed in conversation, in letters, printed essays, or the elementary books of public right, as Aristotle, Cicero, Locke, Sidney &c."

Most importantly the Declaration was an inflection point in global history. Western history is replete with lists of duties and obligations, expressed or implied, due from every category of citizen under written or traditional forms of princely or ecclesiastical rule. As Algernon Sidney mockingly put it, God "caused some to be born with crowns upon their heads, and all others with saddles upon their backs."

The Declaration aspires to make the last first.

Abraham Lincoln. Colorized photograph by Mathew Brady.

Source: Wikimedia

Epilogue

The elegant simplicity of it all is what strikes me most.

Do unto others, or in the proscriptive legal sense Do not unto others…. Give to a person what is due to that person. Seek happiness. All are free and equal. All have a right to be part of the consent of the governed. All have fundamental rights to freedom of speech, worship, thought and conscience, among others. The people are sovereign. Those who govern are accountable to the people. The people retain a right of revolution, but not of subversion or rebellion.

The unwritten but implied clause is that because the people created government, individually and collectively the people are ultimately responsible for it. Were that not true there would be no reason for me to write this essay nor for you to read it. The challenge isn't that some hyper-partisan group will snatch democracy away from us all; it is that we will allow that to happen. Not to act on this score would be to forsake every soul who has contributed to and defended our national creed — those concepts that have been honed and polished over centuries of trial and conflict, like stones smoothed to a sheen in a clear creek bed.

George Washington took the presidential oath of office in April 1789. The American experiment was underway, guided initially by voices of the moderate Enlightenment.

During the same year a revolution broke out in France that changed the face of Europe. Radical Enlightenment thinking guided its development. Denis Diderot, who did as much as any person to spread the faith of reason warned of the dangers lurking among the masses, of their "wickedness, stupidity, inhumanity, unreason and prejudice." Baron d'Holbach, Diderot's friend and collaborator, amplified the warning, saying "Of all tyrannies, democratic tyranny is the cruelest and least rational." He could not have known how right he was.

The French Revolution proclaimed using reason's outer boundaries as the wellspring of governance. Terror became the instrument of liberty, equality, and fraternity. The guillotine settled disagreements. In the following century Adolph Hitler distorted reason into strands of pure evil under fascism's banner. The result was the Holocaust. Nuclear weapons and artificial intelligence, just now emerging, are exercises in following pure reason to its logical conclusions.

Reason, the antidote to suffocating ecclesiasticism, can be a direct path to hell.

So, what about the Declaration, surely an ark of hope?

The Declaration is an 18th century document. Its assertion of natural rights is an anachronism. When it was enacted the philosopher Jeremy Bentham complained that the term 'natural rights' was "simply nonsense," and invoking 'inalienable rights' was "nonsense on stilts." More recently the scholar Thomas West has offered the bleak conclusion that "for more than two centuries, people have increasingly believed that human reasoning cannot lead to universally true principles of natural rights, but only to an awareness of the historical contingency of all claims to truth." Or, as Ecclesiastes puts it, "time and chance happeneth."

If we are to embrace historical contingency over self-evident truths then state constitutions citing the natural rights they are intended to protect need to be rewritten in Massachusetts, Vermont, Pennsylvania, New York, Virginia, New Hampshire, Delaware, North Carolina and Rhode Island.

The irony is that rights revealed by right reason were undermined by reason itself. By the late 19th century, a more strictly reasoned account of rights had overtaken natural rights. A right that is unenforceable is ephemeral. Rights are made enforceable by laws. Courts must cite statutes rather than self-evident truths in declaring judgments.

On the one hand, the Declaration is the first entry in the statute book of federal laws. It is included in the U.S. Code as one of the nation's organic laws. On the other hand, it is not legally binding. Recourse to it is common as the ultimate expression of a national creed. In imagination it is the sacred ground where patriots rally.

In the millennium's second decade, rejection of parts of the Declaration is common in public demonstrations and in state legislation.

Abraham Lincoln likened pre-Civil War America to a house divided against itself between freedom and slavery. He predicted that the house would not fall. Instead, he believed it would become all one thing, or all the other: either all free or all slave. We are now at a similar junction in our history as a nation divided between whether or not it will accept or reject a transition to more autocratic rule.

Legislative suppression of the vote of minority communities or a particular political party openly mocks the concept of equality. A person who is barred from voting does not live in a democracy. Ranks of marchers shouting their antisemitic slogan "You shall not replace us" are not voicing support for a social contract under which all are equal. Threatening or actually committing political violence, as Dr. Martin Luther King Jr. taught this country, is anathema to freedom. The Confederate flag symbolizes the worst breech of our social contract in the nation's history. The Stars and Bars stand for white supremacy as much now as it did then. Carrying that flag through the halls of Congress during an insurrection was an act of contempt for the Declaration's assertion of universal equality, and the Constitution's provisions to secure the peaceful transfer of power. For millions of Americans, our social contract is not just under strain, it is broken. It will not serve to simply observe, record or lament this fact. Unless this generation affirms our political creed, as past generations have done, the principles of democracy will slip through our fingers like golden grains of sand. We can cry over the loss or cry out to prevent it.

History does not move backwards. Repairing to some past condition of presumed harmony is naïve. Allowing the system to break apart would an admission that the American experiment has floundered because a sufficient number of its own people no longer believe in it.

Social researchers Steven Levitsky and Lucan Way project that "The United States appears headed toward endemic regime instability. Such a scenario would be marked by frequent constitutional crises, including contested or stolen elections and severe conflict between presidents and Congress (such as impeachments and executive efforts to bypass Congress), the judiciary (such as efforts to purge or pack the courts), and state governments (such as intense battles over voting rights and the administration of elections).

"The United States would likely shift back and forth between periods of dysfunctional democracy and periods of competitive authoritarian rule during which incumbents abuse state power, tolerate or encourage violent extremism, and tilt the electoral playing field against their rivals."

In November 1863 Abraham Lincoln visited the Gettysburg battlefield in Pennsylvania to deliver a few closing remarks at the dedication of the soldiers' cemetery there. He explained why the Civil War was being fought and issued a challenge to those who could hear or read his words.

He chose the Declaration as the framework for what he wanted to say. Our forebearers had created a new nation, he said, "conceived in Liberty, and dedicated to the proposition that all men are created equal." Lincoln's trust in the Declaration was marrow deep. He ran a Senate campaign a few years earlier urging Illinois voters to hold fast to the Declaration's principles over the sophistry of dismissing slavery's expansion as a purely local decision of no national import. It was "altogether fitting and proper," the president said, to dedicate a portion of the battlefield as a "final resting place for those who here gave their lives that that nation might live."

He then challenged his audience. The soldiers who had given "their last full measure of devotion" had already dedicated their final resting place "far above our poor power to add or detract." It was rather for "us the living … to be here dedicated to the great task remaining before us … that we here highly resolve … that government of the people, by the people, for the people, shall not perish from the earth."

For us the living … to be here dedicated. Lincoln's challenge is as surely directed to those alive today as to those alive then.

The Declaration was then and remains today the ark of our hopes, the expression of 'the better angels of our nature,' and the aim of our future, if we will but make it so.

About The Author

Ben McNitt has pursued careers in journalism, including being CNN's Cairo Bureau Chief and Middle East correspondent in the later 1980s, environmental advocacy with the National Wildlife Federation in Washington, D.C., and custom woodworking at his current home. He lives on a patch of the Sonoran Desert north of Tucson. His first book is *A House Divided Slavery and American Politics from the Constitution to the Civil War*.